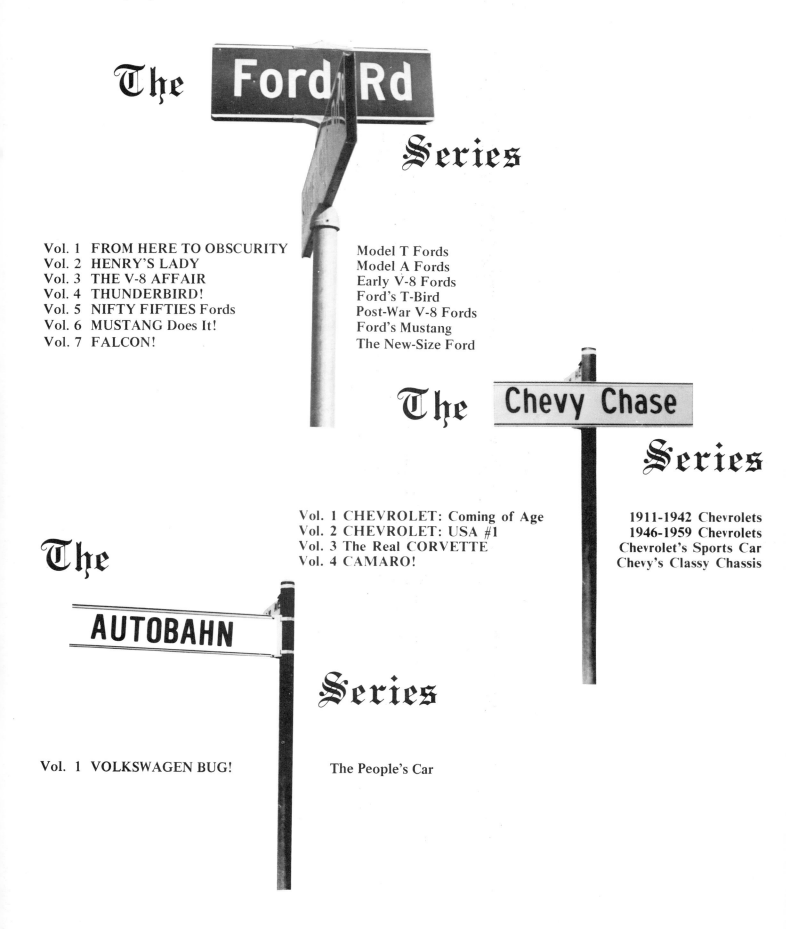

The Ford Rd Series

Vol. 1   FROM HERE TO OBSCURITY   Model T Fords
Vol. 2   HENRY'S LADY   Model A Fords
Vol. 3   THE V-8 AFFAIR   Early V-8 Fords
Vol. 4   THUNDERBIRD!   Ford's T-Bird
Vol. 5   NIFTY FIFTIES Fords   Post-War V-8 Fords
Vol. 6   MUSTANG Does It!   Ford's Mustang
Vol. 7   FALCON!   The New-Size Ford

The Chevy Chase Series

Vol. 1 CHEVROLET: Coming of Age   1911-1942 Chevrolets
Vol. 2 CHEVROLET: USA #1   1946-1959 Chevrolets
Vol. 3 The Real CORVETTE   Chevrolet's Sports Car
Vol. 4 CAMARO!   Chevy's Classy Chassis

The AUTOBAHN Series

Vol. 1 VOLKSWAGEN BUG!   The People's Car

FIRST PRINTING
March 1972

TWELFTH PRINTING
November 1994

THE V8 AFFAIR

AN ILLUSTRATED HISTORY OF THE PRE-WAR FORD V-8

By Ray Miller

THE EVERGREEN PRESS
P.O. Box 306 Avalon California 90704

THE V8 AFFAIR

an illustrated history of the pre-war Ford V-8

ISBN 0-913056-02-2

Library of Congress Catalog Card Number 70-174898

Copyright © 1972, by Ray Miller

Printed by:

Sierra Printers, Inc.
Bakersfield, California

GLENN EMBREE, well known to readers of **The Vintage Ford,** served as President of the Model T Ford Club of America and has provided the colorful covers for their magazine since its inception. Fundamentally a Photographic Essayist, Glenn has been involved with photography both as a hobby and Profession since 1940.

His Studio, in Hollywood, California, is adorned with his portraits of the famous and near-famous, and his work in the field of advertising illustrations has been well applauded. It was Glenn who shot the illustrations for the first four-seated Thunderbirds in 1957, and he has had a long-continuing relationship with the Ford Motor Company in whose current Mustang advertisements Glenn's illustrations often appear. He is a craftsman who unique talent with a lens produced the outstanding illustrations contained in this book.

RAY MILLER, along with Bruce McCalley, another Founding Member of the Model T Ford Club of America, produced **From Here To Obscurity**, a book that has become the Standard Reference for those interested in the Model T Ford. From this effort, it was a relatively modest step to apply similar techniques of reporting to the pre-war Ford V-8 and this book is the result.

Owner, in pre-war years, of several Fords, including a '33 Coupe and a '36 Sedan, his interest in the car was rekindled several years ago when he acquired and restored a 1936 DeLuxe Phaeton. This car is now driven daily in nearby Oceanside, California, where he now makes his home.

In addition to the responsibility for the text and the production of this book, it was Ray who located the outstanding array of beautifully maintained cars used to illustrate this work.

THE

an illustrated

AFFAIR

history of the pre-war Ford V-8

By Ray Miller

With Photographs by Glenn Embree

The Authors wish to thank those whose interest in this project was expressed by their encouragement and cooperation. Needless to say, the owners of the cars featured are especially thanked, for without their help this Journal could never have been completed. In addition, we also wish to thank:

The FORD MOTOR COMPANY for their permission to reprint selected portions of their 1938 Service Manual.

The EARLY FORD V-8 CLUB OF AMERICA, and its President, Mr. Gordon Chamberlin, for his encouragement, advice, and aid. The Club's action, in making time available to us at their Western National Meet in Portland in the Fall of 1971, greatly advanced the progress of this book.

Mr. Carl Burnett, of Antique Automotive in San Diego, and Mr. Gene Valdes, Ford Parts Obsolete in Long Beach, California, both of whom opened their vast inventories to our camera and aided us both in identifying and in obtaining specific parts for our photographic essays.

In preparing this material, the authors have attempted to locate surviving unrestored original automobiles, where possible. Failing in this, we have employed, as models, restorations of the highest quality. Our gratitude is extended to the owners of these cars.

As is to be expected, there may well be items of incorrect date or style on any given automobile. Original cars may have been modified for any number of reasons by their owners; restorations are generally done to the best level of information available to the restorer, but occasionally a slip-up, sometimes of frightening proportions, will occur.

We have attempted to screen the inaccuracies; we hope that we may have succeeded in this attempt. This book was intended to be what it is, a copendium of information which will enable an observer to identify and to classify both cars and component parts. If there are errors, they are not to our knowledge.

The Authors

In a photograph taken in Newark, New Jersey, in May of 1940, the author's "new" 1933 Coupe is inspected by his younger sister and friend.

The Author's **affaire de coeur** with the "flathead" Ford V-8 began in Asbury Park, New Jersey in 1940 during his seventeenth summer. A dusty seven-year-old three window coupe, with a rumble seat, became his prized possession as a high school graduation gift from his parents. Distinctly recalled, even now, was the cost, all of seventy-five dollars, a huge sum in those halcyon days just before the War.

Tan in color, and with shiny stainless steel trim, the perky little '33 Coupe quickly became the family "pet", and spent that summer commuting from the beach to the lakes to the stores, and to the railroad station to pick up Dad after his long week in the City. Easy to park and to steer, the little coupe had one well recalled quirk: the accelerator, hinged as it was, at the top, would tend to pound down hard when the car hit a bump or crossed a railroad track. As I recall, it took several days after I owned the car to make peace with the beastie over this matter.

I now recall this little '33 as a friend to whom I was unfaithful. Attempting to drive from New Brunswick to Williamsburg, Virginia, during the Fall of 1941, and failing to heed its warning knocks, I burned out a connecting rod bearing and shortly after, sheared the rod to put an end through the oil pan not unlike the world's most horrible compound fracture. Limping into Washington, D.C. at 2:00 A.M., we found our way to an all-night garage where a mechanic assured me that all "would be well in the morning".

That next day, I **willingly** let the mechanic buy the car for the estimated cost of the repairs and the sum of only $15 cash! Very shortly thereafter came Pearl Harbor and the total conversion of the automobile industry to war production and a consequent automobile shortage. Never since has the Ford V-8 been worth so little!

So, it is with some little nostalgia, and some great affection, that we now begin...

THE   V-8   AFFAIR

The Authors wish to give thanks to the Owners of cars featured in this work. No attempt has been made to isolate these cars, rather, since we have been endeavoring to describe the characteristics of a given year, we have deliberately employed those pictures which best served our immediate purpose. For this reason, adjacent photos may not necessarily show views of the same car.

CONTENTS

1932

1933

 1934

1935 **1936**

1937

1940

1938

1941

1939

1942

Photo courtesy of Ford Archives,
Henry Ford Museum, Dearborn, Michigan

FORD MOTOR COMPANY

HISTORY: Originally incorporated under the laws of Michigan, June 16, 1903, and capitalized for $100,000, of which only $28,000 in cash was actually paid in. There were twelve stockholders, including Henry Ford, who held 25% of the stock. Later, in 1906, Mr. Ford acquired sufficient stock to bring his holdings up to 51%, and shortly thereafter purchased an additional 7½%. This arrangement continued until 1919, when Edsel B. Ford, who had succeeded his father as president, purchased the remaining 41½% of outstanding stock. The present Ford Motor Co. was incorporated July 9, 1919 under the laws of Delaware, with an authorized capital stock of $100,000,000. During years 1919 and 1920 present company acquired all assets of predecessor.

The Ford Motor Co. sold its first car in July, 1903, and during its first fiscal year produced 1,708 cars. During the first five years it built and sold approximately 25,000 Ford cars of various models, and on Oct. 1, 1908, produced the first Model T Ford car. It was seven years later, December 10, 1915, when Model T Motor No. 1,000,000 was produced. Model T No. 10,000,000 was produced on June 4, 1924, and No. 15,000,000 on May 26, 1927. Manufacture of the Model T car ceased with the production of No. 15,000,000, except for service parts to care for the repair requirements of approximately 9,000,000 Model T cars then in use. Retooling of the Ford plants for the production of a new car, then already under way, began on a general scale, and on October 20, 1927, the first new Model A engine came off the engine assembly line at the Rouge plant and the same day was assembled into a new car. The new Model A car was formally announced to the public Nov. 28, 1927, and was given its first public showing on December 2, 1927. On Mar. 31, 1932 initial public showing was made of the improved "4" and the new "V-8" cars.

1933 MOODY'S MANUAL OF INVESTMENTS, page 2765

PREFACE

Things were different in those days.

The Stock Market had "crashed" in October of 1929, and the Country had panicked. The Administration, headed by Herbert Hoover, was trying feverishly to stem the oncoming tide of economic disaster. It was, perhaps, too early for us all to foretell the chaotic times which were to befall us, but the signs were there to be seen.

This was the start of the "Depression Years". The times, now almost forgotten, when unemployment was everywhere. Workers fought for jobs as they never had and never have since. In Detroit, it was said, auto workers were forced to **pay** up to three quarters of their day's wages just for the privilege of working! Police were employed to maintain order in employment lines, and the migratory workers in California's Imperial Valley counted themselves fortunate to earn $40 per month !

The Nation **needed** new stimuli and its leaders sought everywhere for such. Perhaps this was the reason that Henry Ford chose this most unlikely time of all, March of 1932, to herald the introduction of his newest creation. For March, especially in the East is an unhospitable month. Winter seems to hold its grasp on the area and it is rare that the weather works to warm and stimulate the residents.

Into this unlikely environment, on March 31, 1932, was thrust the "new Ford Eight", not yet firmly entrenched as the "Ford V-8". That Henry Ford was again right in his judgement, appears obvious. Once again he had picked a "winner", for the records show that he was to go on to build over six million cars with this basic engine before the War, and as many again after, until substantially revising it in 1954, and at this writing, the Company is still building the direct descendents of the early "Ford V-eight cylinder" engine.

19

4,000,000
3,000,000
2,000,000
1,000,000

1925   1926   1927   1928

NEW CAR

New Car Registrations

	1926	1927	1928	1929	1930	1931
Auburn Automobile	7,117	9,835	11,153	18,652	13,149	30,952
Auburn	7,117	9,835	11,153	17,853	11,270	29,536
Cord				799	1,879	1,416
Austin					4,354	2,941
Chrysler Motors	353,343	278,152	334,190	344,877	224,581	228,459
Chrysler	129,966	154,234	141,800	84,520	60,908	52,650
DeSoto			14,528	59,614	35,267	28,430
Dodge	223,377	123,918	148,541	115,774	64,105	53,090
Plymouth			29,321	84,969	64,301	94,289
DeVaux						4,808
Durant	91,794	56,781	71,263	47,716	21,440	7,229
Ford Motor Co.	1,196,674	399,884	487,371	1,316,298	1,059,453	532,047
Ford	1,189,004	393,424	481,344	1,310,147	1,055,097	528,581
Lincoln	7,670	6,460	6,027	6,151	4,356	3,466
Franklin	7,173	7,526	7,423	10,704	7,482	3,881
General Motors	896,110	1,115,579	1,295,046	1,271,134	905,427	825,437
Buick	229,597	232,428	195,691	172,307	122,656	90,873
Cadillac-LaSalle	24,735	29,719	36,888	35,226	23,340	18,019
Cadillac	24,735	18,748	18,133	14,936	12,078	11,136
LaSalle		10,971	18,755	20,290	11,262	6,883
Chevrolet	493,852	647,810	767,867	780,014	618,884	583,429
Oakland-Pontiac	99,414	157,049	220,993	190,104	90,037	86,133
Oakland	49,539	41,843	37,168	31,831	21,648	12,985
Pontiac	49,875	115,206	183,825	158,273	68,389	73,148
Oldsmobile	48,512	48,573	73,607	93,483	50,510	46,983
Willys-Overland	142,510	139,406	230,962	199,709	65,766	51,341
Willys	96,848	100,206	191,301	162,366	51,687	42,936
Willys-Knight	45,662	39,200	39,661	37,343	14,079	8,405
Miscellaneous	62,163	51,484	39,708	20,390	4,697	1,880
Total	3,298,933	2,623,538	3,133,399	3,880,247	2,625,979	1,908,141
Total Except Ford and General Motors	1,206,149	1,108,075	1,340,982	1,292,815	661,099	550,657

Registrations, not production figures, actually tell the story. What a factory *produces* isn't really the important thing, its what the customers *buy* that counts. Ford had long been locked in competition with the Chevrolet Division of General Motors and a study of comparative registrations for several years earlier is illuminating. From the issue of AUTOMOTIVE TRADE JOURNAL of April 1st, 1932, comes the story.

Although Ford and Chevrolet each led in total registrations for three of the six years from 1926 through 1931, Chevrolet held a commanding first place in 1931 with 30.60% of the total automobile market, *better than ten per cent* more than Ford.

The records indicate that Ford produced its Model A through March of 1932 (although at a rapidly declining rate). About 2700 were produced in March against over 127,000 a year earlier. The drop in Model A production was programmed though, programmed by Henry Ford to whom figures available a year earlier had determined his course.

SALES TREND
1929 | 1930 | 1931 | 1932
4,000,000
3,000,000
2,000,000
1,000,000

	Per Cent of Total						Rank					
	1926	1927	1928	1929	1930	1931	1926	1927	1928	1929	1930	1931
Auburn Automobile Co.	.22	.37	.35	.49	.50	1.62						
Auburn	.22	.37	.35	.47	.43	1.55	24	24	25	23	24	13
Cord				.02	.07	.07				31	31	31
Austin					.17	.15					29	30
Chrysler Motors	10.71	10.60	10.65	8.87	8.53	11.96						
Chrysler	3.94	5.88	4.51	2.18	2.32	2.76	6	5	8	11	8	7
DeSoto			.46	1.54	1.34	1.49			24	15	13	14
Dodge	6.77	4.72	4.74	2.96	2.43	2.78	4	6	7	7	6	6
Plymouth			.94	2.19	2.44	4.95			19	10	5	3
DeVaux						.25						26
Durant	2.79	2.17	2.29	1.23	.82	.38	10	12	12	16	19	22
Ford Motor	36.27	15.25	15.54	33.92	40.34	27.87						
Ford	36.04	15.00	15.35	33.76	40.17	27.69	1	2	2	1	1	2
Lincoln	.23	.25	.19	.16	.17	.18	22	26	28	29	28	29
Franklin	.22	.29	.25	.29	.28	.20	23	25	27	26	26	28
General Motors	27.13	42.53	41.34	32.79	34.48	43.28						
Buick	6.95	8.86	6.25	4.45	4.67	4.77	3	3	3	4	3	4
Cadillac-LaSalle	.75	1.13	1.18	.90	.89	.94						
Cadillac	.75	.71	.58	.38	.46	.58	19	19	22	25	22	20
LaSalle		.42	.60	.52	.43	.36		21	21	22	25	23
Chevrolet	14.95	24.70	24.51	20.12	23.56	30.60	2	1	1	2	2	1
Oakland-Pontiac	3.01	5.99	7.05	4.89	3.43	4.51						
Oakland	1.50	1.60	1.19	.82	.82	.68	12	14	18	20	18	19
Pontiac	1.51	4.39	5.86	4.07	2.61	3.83	13	7	5	6	4	5
Oldsmobile	1.47	1.85	2.35	2.42	1.93	2.46	14	13	11	9	12	8
Studebaker Corp.	3.03	3.83	3.59	2.35	2.41	2.68						
Pierce-Arrow	.17	.22	.18	.21	.26	.24	25	27	29	27	27	27
Studebaker	2.86	3.61	3.41	2.14	2.15	2.44	9	10	10	12	9	9
Stutz	.12	.11	.08	.07	.03	.02	27	28	30	30	32	33
Willys-Overland	4.32	5.32	7.37	5.14	2.52	2.69						
Willys	2.94	3.82	6.10	4.18	1.98	2.25	8	9	4	5	10	10
Willys-Knight	1.38	1.50	1.27	.96	.54	.44	15	15	17	19	20	21
Miscellaneous	1.90	1.96	1.26	.52	.18	.10						
Total	100.00	100.00	100.00	100.00	100.00	100.00						
Total Except Ford and Gen. Motors	36.60	42.28	43.12	33.29	25.18	28.85						

It was apparent to all that Ford had to come up with a new car; new from the ground up. Despite the fabulous initial popularity of Ford's Model A (which unbelievably, had sold almost three million cars in its first three years!), in its later years, Model A was being unsuccessfully compared to more sophisticated cars of other contemporary manufacturers and thus seen to be lacking.

Having correctly predicted the need to upgrade the Model T after almost twenty years of production, the giant Ford Motor Company again discerned the need to upgrade after only four years of Model A. Since early 1934 when the new V-8 model was displayed, and with the exception of the war years of 1943-45, there has been a "new model" placed in production every year and the trend shows no signs of turning, despite the fact that the *basic* characteristics of the Ford V-8 have actually only been superficially altered in the intervening 40 years.

ANNOUNCING THE NEW FORD
V-8 Cylinder

THE NEW FORD EIGHT *De Luxe Tudor Sedan*

Eight-cylinder, 90-degree V-type, 65-horse-power Engine * Vibrationless
Roomy, Beautiful Bodies * Low Center of Gravity * Silent Second Gear
Synchronized Silent Gear Shift * Seventy-five Miles per Hour * Comfortable
Riding Springs * Rapid Acceleration * Low Gasoline Consumption * Reliability

New self-adjusting Houdaille double-acting hydraulic shock absorbers with thermostatic control . . . New rear spring construction . . . Automatic spark control . . . Down-draft carburetor . . . Carburetor silencer . . . Bore, 3 1/16 inches. Stroke, 3 3/4 inches . . . Piston displacement, 221 cubic inches . . .

90-degree counterbalanced crankshaft . . . Large, effective fully enclosed four-wheel brakes . . . Distinctive steel-spoke wheels with large hub caps . . . Handsome V-type radiator . . . Graceful new roof line and slanting windshield of clear polished plate safety glass . . . Single-bar bumpers, chromium plated . . . Low, drop

center frame . . . Mechanically operated pump drawing fuel from fourteen-gallon gasoline tank in rear . . . Choke on instrument panel . . . Individual inside sun visors . . . Cowl ventilation . . . Adjustable driver's seat . . . Choice of Mohair, Broadcloth or Bedford Cord upholstery in all de luxe closed types.

THE NEW FORD FOUR-CYLINDER CAR

An improved Ford four-cylinder, 50-horse-power engine, operating with new smoothness, is available in the fourteen body types listed below.

A GREAT NEW CAR AT AN UNUSUALLY LOW PRICE ** FOURTEEN BODY TYPES

Roadster	Tudor Sedan	Sport Coupe	De Luxe Roadster	De Luxe Tudor	Cabriolet	Victoria
Phaeton	Coupe	Fordor Sedan	De Luxe Phaeton	De Luxe Coupe	De Luxe Fordor	Convertible Sedan

Ford

GET COMPLETE INFORMATION AND PRICES THURSDAY, MARCH 31, AT ALL FORD DEALERS

"I shall build a car for the masses", said Henry Ford. To many his determined statement was satisfied by the Model T Ford, over 15,000,000 of which were produced by 1927. Surely there would never again be an automobile with anything like the acceptance of that patriach of the Ford motor car line. Millions purchased the established Model T. Their sons and daughters continued, and over the course of nineteen years of production and Henry Ford's words would indeed appear to have been prophetic.

Then came a totally new car; one so new in appearance, power plant, style, comfort, and ahead of its time. Again there were those who would say, "he made good his promise". Certainly, the manufacture and sale of almost three and one-half million more cars in the brief four years of Model A's life would justify such a belief. But perhaps Henry Ford in his mischievous way, had something else in mind when he uttered his promise.

Model V-8 was formally introduced in March of 1932. Seeming at first to be merely a new eight cylinder, vee-type engine packaged in a body similar in appearance to Model A, there were many who overlooked the significance of the event. Regardless, America was then embarked on an exciting automotive binge and this first "primitive" Ford V-8 engine became the first of a common line, unbroken (except for the War) that would last until 1954! Twenty-two years were to follow in which the basic power plant of the Ford motor car would be relatively unchanged!

America, in its desire for the new, for the different, for the "better", went on a buying spree. Purchasers eagerly sought the "next year's model" and people everywhere became conditioned by advertising and their environment to dispose of the old and acquire the new. True, changes were made; many of them essential, but many of them appearance changes only. Fundamentally, the differences in the V-8 models from year to year were largely in its appearance, and these changes contributed little to the improvement of the basic item, a reliable, rugged, sturdy, and comfortable vehicle...above all...

"...a car for the masses..."

AUTOMOBILE TRADE JOURNAL

With Which is Combined MOTOR AGE

Established 1896

Copyright 1932 by Chilton Class Journal Company

VOL. XXXVII   NO. 5

PHILADELPHIA, APRIL 1, 1932

In This Issue

The April, 1932, issue of THE AUTOMOBILE TRADE JOURNAL was among the very first with a professional analysis of the new Ford Eight. The article was apparently a last-minute addition to the issue for it neither appeared in the table of contents (above) nor was it printed in correctly sequential pages. The entire four page article, reproduced here, appeared on pages thoughtfully numbered 32A through 32D and was unlisted in the magazine.

PRICES

	New V-8	New Four	Old Model A	Last Model T
Roadster	$460	$410	$430	$360
Phaeton	495	445	435	380
Tudor Sedan	500	450	490	495
Coupe	490	440	490	485
Sport Coupe	535	485	500	...
Fordor Sedan	590	540	590	545
DeLuxe Roadster	500	450	475	...
DeLuxe Phaeton	545	495	580	...
DeLuxe Tudor Sedan	550	500	525	...
DeLuxe Coupe	575	525	525	...
Cabriolet	610	560	595	...
DeLuxe Fordor Sedan	645	595	630	...
Victoria	600	550	580	...
Convertible Sedan	650	600	640	...

New FORD 8

75 m.p.h. with new 65 hp. Vee-engine —50 hp. improved four-cylinder engine available in same chassis— Wheelbase 106 in.

WITH a new 65 hp., 90-deg. V-eight and an improved 50 hp. four-cylinder model, Ford again is in a position to offer the strongest kind of competition for the low-priced market. Except for the engines, there is practically no difference between the two lines of cars as the 106-in. wheelbase chassis and body models are substantially alike. Prices are given in the accompanying table.

The new eight-cylinder engine has a 3 1/16-in. bore and 3¾-in. stroke, giving it a displacement of 221 cu. in. It develops its peak horsepower of 65 at 3400 r.p.m. and, it is said, gives the car a top speed of 75 m.p.h. No details are available on the improved four-cylinder powerplant, but it is understood that its bore and stroke are the same as the Model A, the increase in horsepower from 40 to 50 being the result of refinements in design.

Both cars are available in 14 body styles which are featured by slanting, visorless windshields of safety glass, well-curved roof lines at front and rear, adjustable drivers' seats, inside adjustable sunshades, lower overall height and V-type radiators. The increase in the wheelbase from 103½ to 106 in., of course, has made it possible to make all bodies roomier.

The new chassis embodies a number of interesting features such as silent synchronized gear shift with silent gears, new chassis spring construction, self-adjusting

Houdaille shock absorbers, newly designed four-wheel brakes with 186 sq. in. of braking area, electrically welded steel spoke wheels, double-drop frame which conforms to the shape of the body, and the chassis and running gear are cushioned by rubber insulators in the spring shackles and shock-absorber links. Bodies are insulated from the frame by rubber pads. The drive is of the torque-tube type with hollow propeller shaft. Tires are 18 x 5.25 in.

Cylinders and crankcase of the new eight are in one unit. A counterweighted crankshaft, with crank throws at 90 deg. to each other, provides running balance. Main bearings are approximately 2 in. in diameter and there is a flange on each cap which fits into a corresponding groove in the case to assure alignment. Crankshaft is offset

FORDOR

TUDOR

ROADSTER

VICTORIA

TUDOR

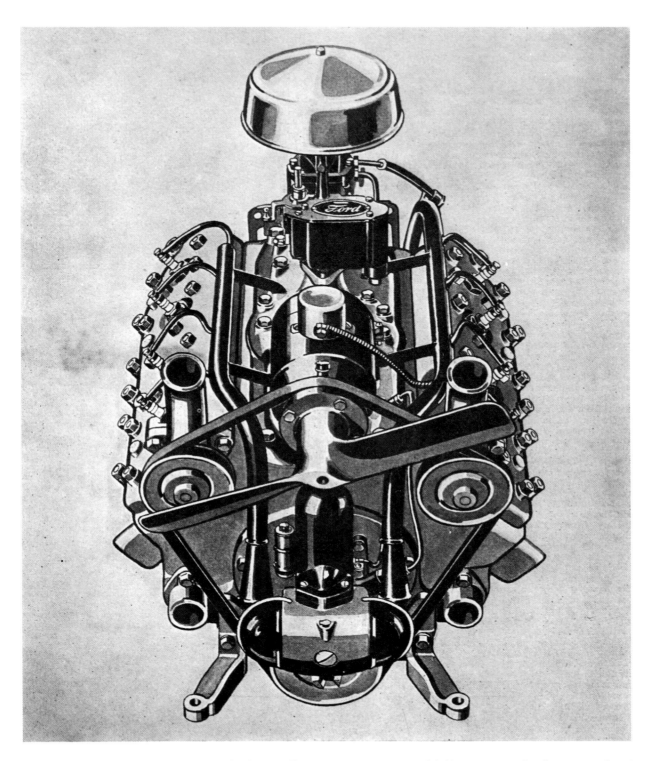

New Ford V-8 engine. Combination coil and distributor are mounted at front of engine and driven directly from camshaft. V-belt drives two water pumps, fan and generator

3/16 in. relative to center lines of cylinder bores. Compression ratio is 5.5 to 1. To reduce the transmission of vibration, rubber engine mountings have been adopted for both the new four and eight.

Connecting rods are mounted side by side on the crankpins and have an unusual type bearing which consists of a split sleeve babbitted on both sides. This sleeve rides on the crankpin and the connecting rod rides on the outer surface of the sleeve. The internal diameter of this sleeve is 2 in. while the external measures 2¼ in. approximately.

Main, connecting rod and camshaft bearings are pressure-lubricated. Pistons are of aluminum alloy and have three rings. Pins are retained in the same manner as on the Model A and are ¾ in. in diameter.

Valves are also of new design. These valves have mushroom ends which are much larger than the ends of the Model A valves and ride directly on the cam. In this way the conventional valve-lifting mechanism is eliminated. There is no adjustment for valve clearance. Valve head clear diameter is 1⅜ in.

A cast aluminum plate which covers the angle between the cylinder blocks incorporates the intake manifold. On top of this plate is mounted the downdraft carburetor with intake silencer. Fuel from the 14 gal. supply tank at the rear of the car is forced to the carburetor by means of a fuel pump located on the cover plate, close to the carburetor.

The carburetor bears the manufacturer's label by Detroit Lubricator Co. There are no external mixture adjustments. The mixture control is by a needle valve placed in the center of the vertical air-intake. An accelerating pump is provided. An air intake silencer is standard.

Gravity feed of gasoline used on Model A has been abandoned in favor of a rear-mounted 14-gal. gasoline tank. Gasoline is supplied to the carburetor by a diaphragm type pump which is mounted at the rear of the combination intake manifold and valve cover plate assembly.

Force feed lubrication is supplied to main, connecting rod and camshaft bearings by an oil pump driven from the camshaft by an idler gear, at the rear of the crankcase. Oil from the pump flows under 20 to 25 lb. pressure to the rear camshaft bearing, thence through a deep groove to the rear main bearing. Here another groove admits oil to the hollow crankshaft with leads to the crankpin. Oil also flows from the pump through a horizontal tube extending the length of the engine above the camshaft, distributing oil to the center and front camshaft bearings where the distribution to main bearings and crankpins is repeated in the same fashion as the rear camshaft and main bearings. The camshaft is mounted in the bottom of the V and is driven by a non-metallic gear from the crankshaft.

The ignition unit is bolted to the front of the engine and is driven directly from the front end of the camshaft without intermediate gears. Automatic advance with vacuum control is provided. It is removable for attention to the breaker-points. The coupling to the shaft insures correct timing when the unit is replaced. The distributor is of unusual design with the distributor-arms revolving at right angles to distributor caps instead of in a plane parallel therewith. High tension current from a Mallory coil is carried in concealed wiring to a brush contacting a copper ring on the shaft. Two arms on the shaft contact two points on one distributor cap and two points on the distributor cap on the opposite side of the unit. There is provision for changing the timing in the unit plus or minus 7 deg. Champion Model C4 spark plugs are standard equipment. Firing order is one, five, four, eight, six, three, seven, two, number one cylinder being right forward and number five being left forward.

A single V-type fan belt drives both of the water pumps and the fan, the generator being driven from an extension of the fan shaft.

There is a water pump at the top of each cylinder block with a relatively large outlet and hose extending to the radiator. Pumps are of centrifugal type and there is space enough to permit thermo-syphon cooling should the pump be put out of action by a broken belt. There are no stuffing boxes on the pump shafts and leakage is prevented by spring-loaded packing.

Intake and exhaust ports are cored in the cylinder blocks. The intake passages in the valve cover plate are surrounded, as previously stated, by an exhaust heated hot-spot supplied by the two center cylinders on each side. Exhaust from these cylinders, after entering the hot-spot chamber, is discharged from a port into an exhaust manifold bolted to the outside of the block. Exhaust from the front and rear cylinders, on each block, is carried to the exhaust manifold through a passage in the block. Exhaust pipes are attached to the front of the exhaust manifold, that on the right sweeping downward under the side pan and that on the left being carried around front of the engine and joining exhaust pipe on the right under the pan.

The engine, which weighs 581 lb. without the transmission, is supported at the front on two-angle "feet." Under each of these supports is placed a 2 in. rubber ball put under compression by a bolt. The rear mounting is a large moulded rubber trunnion incorporated in the vertical section of a center cross-member which is placed at the rear of the transmission. There is no metal contact between engine and frame. Two "stabilizers," which are steel rods, extend from the cross-member to flat surfaces on the crankcase, where engine arms ordinarily would be placed. These rods are to prevent forward motion of the engine in the rubber supports during sudden brake applications.

The front axle is similar in design to the Model A and the front double radius rod "wish-bone" is retained, but it is fastened at the rear to the same center cross-member at the rear of the transmission which contains the rubber rear engine mounting. This construction avoids breaking transmission case in event of front end collision. Rear end of the wish-bone terminates in a ball, as on Model A, and is insulated by rubber.

Transmission has three speeds forward, with silent second provided by helical gears for the countershaft and second speed gears. There is a synchronizing mechanism for second and high which embodies a tapered collar with internal-external gear type clutch. Clutch is of the plate type and is cushioned by helical springs.

There is no free-wheeling mechanism, nor vacuum operated clutch, contrary to preliminary gossip on the subject.

Transverse springs are used both front and rear with rubber insulation, and therefore, oilless shackles. The front spring is similar to the Model A, but the rear spring is placed behind the axle housing, instead of directly above it, as in Model A. The spring enters the open bottom of a cross-member and extends to brackets extending backwards on the axle housing.

Rear axle is similar in design to Model A except that the driveshaft is tubular. The rear axle ratio is 4.33 to 1.

The frame side rails incorporate a double drop and also bends to match the contour of bodies. The frame at its deepest section measures 6 in., the flange varies in width with an approximate 2 in. maximum. Stock is 3/32 in. For added strength the lower edge of the side rail flares out. There are five cross-members, although casual observers will count four. The odd member is a large V-shaped assembly at the rear of the frame which performs the incidental function of carrying the spare tire. Other cross-members are at the rear spring, at rear of transmission, forming third engine support, a member at the front of the engine and a straight tubular member at the front of the frame.

Brakes are of double-shoe type somewhat like the Model A, but with changes in detail. Drums are of cast iron with an external rib and braking surface measures 12 in. in diameter and 1½ in. in width. Total brake braking surface is 186 sq. in. Both pedal and hand lever operate the same four brakes. The brake cross-shaft does not extend to the frame side rails but is about 6 in. long and attached to the rear of the cross-member which carries the rear engine support. Brake rods extend on an angle from arms from this shaft to the brake camshaft arms.

Brake and clutch pedals are not attached to the engine but are carried on brackets on the center cross-member.

Dash board instruments are compactly arranged in the center. There are three dials, the left being the ammeter, the center dial an 80-mile speedometer with clock hand, and on the right is the hydro-static gasoline gage. Throttle control is by button at the left of the ammeter, the choke button below the speedometer and the dash light button is placed near the gasoline gage. There is no manual spark control. Steering gear is locked for parking by a coincidental lock on the ignition.

To return to the appearance of the car, a V-shaped grille is placed in front of the radiator. This grille is finished in French gray, while the radiator shell is finished to match the body. Rustless steel beading is used to improve the appearance of the radiator shell, while an arched chrome-plated tie-rod connects the head lamps which are of rustless steel. The steel running boards are wide and have the rubber mats vulcanized directly to the steel.

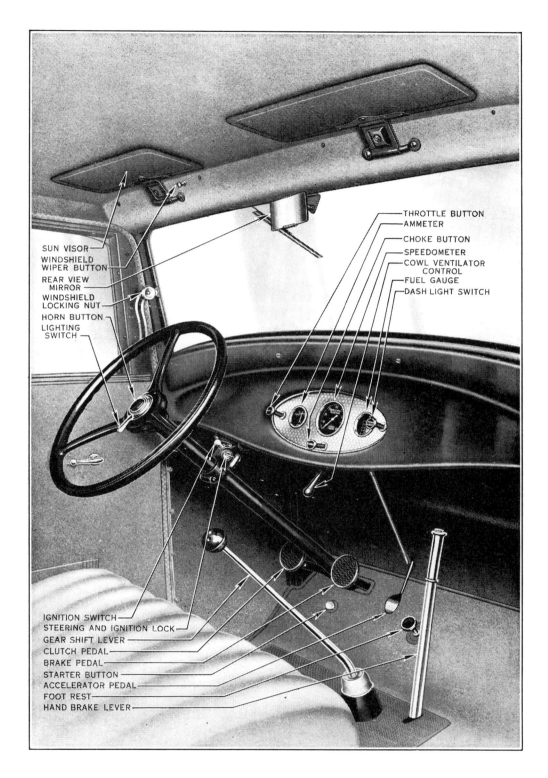

SUN VISOR
WINDSHIELD WIPER BUTTON
REAR VIEW MIRROR
WINDSHIELD LOCKING NUT
HORN BUTTON
LIGHTING SWITCH

THROTTLE BUTTON
AMMETER
CHOKE BUTTON
SPEEDOMETER
COWL VENTILATOR CONTROL
FUEL GAUGE
DASH LIGHT SWITCH

IGNITION SWITCH
STEERING AND IGNITION LOCK
GEAR SHIFT LEVER
CLUTCH PEDAL
BRAKE PEDAL
STARTER BUTTON
ACCELERATOR PEDAL
FOOT REST
HAND BRAKE LEVER

Instruments and Controls of
the 1932 Ford V-8

THE NEW FORD V-8 CYLINDER CAR

FEATURES OF THE NEW FORD V-8

ENGINE—The Ford V-8 engine develops 65 horsepower, which gives the car an unusually high ratio of power to weight. This is one reason why the car is so quick in the getaway and can develop such high speed.

Like all Ford engines, it is simple in design and construction and especially neat in appearance. The two banks of four cylinders each are cast in a single piece with the crankcase, for rigidity and permanent alignment of cylinders. The cylinders are set at an angle of 90 degrees, and the crankshaft, weighing 65 lbs., which is short, stiff, and counterweighted for smooth running, likewise is the 90 degree type.

A new, unique feature of the engine is a one-piece, non-adjustable valve, eliminating the push rod, and contributing to reliability, full power, quietness and economy.

Bore and stroke, $3\frac{1}{16}$ x $3\frac{3}{4}$. Displacement, 221 cubic inches.

ECONOMY—The Ford V-8 is economical in every sense of the word. Its purchase price is low, its running costs reasonable, and its life so long and possible mileage so great as to reduce depreciation to the minimum.

SAFETY—The Ford has always been known as a safe car to ride in, and this feature is heightened in the V-8. The 65-horsepower engine gives you ample power for hills, and the rapid acceleration and easy steering give you unusual maneuverability. Safety glass is used in all windshields. If desired, safety glass may be had in all windows for a small extra charge at time of purchase. The larger four-wheel mechanical brakes enable you to meet the new conditions of speed and power with complete safety. Drums are of special alloy iron, which tests indicate do not easily score. The center of gravity of the car has been lowered, and thus it holds the road, even on rough surfaces and on curves. Transverse springs, torque tube and radius rods, and extra strength in every vital part are some of the additional safety factors.

COMFORT—New riding comfort has been engineered into both the bodies and the chassis. The compactness of the V-8 engine which requires no more space than the 4 cylinder type permits the use of roomy bodies for passenger comfort. The seats are low, and as the center of gravity is also low, you ride with a new sense of ease and security. Cushions are deep and easy. Important improvements have been made in the chassis to increase comfort. The basic Ford principle of transverse springs and low unsprung weight has been retained. The rear spring now is wider, flatter and longer, and a greater proportion of its length is effective in absorbing road shocks. The spring also is now mounted back of the rear axle, which plays a part in lowering the body.

AUTOMATIC SPARK—No spark lever is provided, as no manual adjustment of the spark is required. Spark timing is vacuum controlled, completely automatic, and the spark always occurs at the correct instant for starting, and for smooth power production under all driving conditions.

FUEL PUMP—Ford-designed fuel pump, operated by an eccentric on the camshaft, draws fuel from 14-gallon tank in rear. Accurate fuel gage on dash.

Also an improved 4-cylinder engine

Any of the fourteen beautiful body types is also available, if desired, at a lower price, with an improved 4-cylinder engine. Completely mounted in rubber, the new 4-cylinder engine operates smoothly and quietly. It develops 50 horsepower.

SYNCHRONIZED GEAR SHIFTING—You have probably never driven a car that is so easy to operate as this one. Gear shifting is synchronized with cones between second and high making it possible to shift up or down quickly and without noise, at any speed.

SILENT SECOND—Second speed gears are of the silent helical type, and revolve quietly. This adds greatly to the pleasure of driving.

QUIET OPERATION—Rubber is used at scores of points in the Ford V-8, to absorb and insulate noise and vibration. The engine is mounted at three points in rubber, to provide maximum smoothness of operation. The body is insulated from the frame by rubber pads. There is rubber in the spring shackles, shock absorber connecting links, between the front radius rod and center cross member of the frame, and between the cross member and the torque tube. Body, engine, frame and axles are insulated from each other.

THERMOSTATIC RIDE CONTROL—A thermostatically operated temperature adjustment and a new automatic adjustment to compensate for sudden shocks have been incorporated in the four Houdaille hydraulic double acting shock absorbers. This assures the utmost in riding ease regardless of road conditions or temperatures.

DOUBLE DROP FRAME—The frame has been designed to lower the body, and permit bolting the running boards directly to it, eliminating side dust shields. The V-8 Ford frame has new width, depth and length and is exceptionally light because of improved design and construction. It has five cross members.

LARGER TIRES—The new wheels are smaller, and tires larger, now 18 x 5.25 inches, their added air capacity increasing riding comfort. Hubs are larger, and a beauty detail is the concealment of wheel mounting nuts beneath the hub caps.

We reserve the right to make changes, without notice, in prices, specifications, and equipment at any time without incurring any obligation.

FORD MOTOR COMPANY, DETROIT, MICHIGAN

Photo courtesy of Ford Archives,
Henry Ford Museum, Dearborn, Michigan

1932

Model "18" Ford Passenger Car

BODY TYPE	NAME	BODY TYPE	NAME
PASSENGER			
35	Phaeton (Standard)	55	Tudor Sedan (De Luxe)
35	Phaeton (De Luxe)	68	Cabriolet
40	Roadster (Standard	160	Fordor Sedan (Standard)
40	Roadster (De Luxe)	160	Fordor Sedan (De Luxe)
45	Coupe (Standard)	190	Victoria
50	Coupe (Sport)	400	Convertible Sedan
55	Tudor Sedan (Standard)	520	Coupe (De Luxe)

The Early Ford V-8 engine, in similar fashion to the earliest of the Model T and the Model A engines, differed substantially from the later versions. External differences, more obvious and easier to detect, included the use of a cast-aluminum oil pan and an oil dipstick which was inserted through the right side of the block itself into the pan. There were other differences, for example, the two-bladed fan shown here was shortly replaced by a four-bladed fan designed to move more air.

The generator was mounted on a post, clamped rather than bolted rigidly to the manifold, and the ignition coil appears to have been merely a repackaging of Model A components. An unusual air cleaner, quite different than later varieties, also marks the early assembly.

Although strongly resembling the Model A in appearance, there was a basic difference in the new "Vee-8" cars. Wheelbase had been increased three inches over the Model A's 103" to provide a smoother ride. The increased length allowed for slightly larger bodies from the start, and while they may appear similar to Model A, there were few body parts that might actually interchange.

Lost in the later success of the V-8 engine is the fact that there was also introduced, at this same time, an improved four cylinder engine, the Model B. However, it's popularity was eclipsed and surpassed by the V-8. After 1934, this improved four cylinder engine was dropped.

The V-8 had its early problems. The task of casting, in one piece, an eight cylinder V engine was formidable; heads cracked, the rings at first leaked badly, engine mounts vibrated loose, and so on. Persistent efforts overcame all of the problems, and by 1933 a spectacular finish at the Elgin Stock Car Races resulted in seven Ford V-8's as the first seven finishers! From there on it was smooth sailing for Ford with the only V-8 engine in the low-priced field!

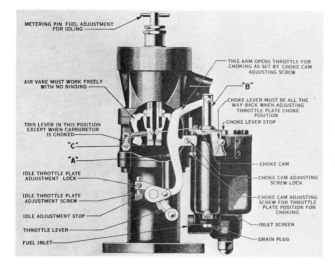

METERING PIN FUEL ADJUSTMENT FOR IDLING

THIS ARM OPENS THROTTLE FOR CHOKING AS SET BY CHOKE CAM ADJUSTING SCREW

"B"

CHOKE LEVER MUST BE ALL THE WAY BACK WHEN ADJUSTING THROTTLE PLATE CHOKE POSITION

CHOKE LEVER STOP

AIR VANE MUST WORK FREELY WITH NO BINDING

THIS LEVER IN THIS POSITION EXCEPT WHEN CARBURETOR IS CHOKED

"C"

"A"

CHOKE CAM

IDLE THROTTLE PLATE ADJUSTMENT LOCK

CHOKE CAM ADJUSTING SCREW LOCK

IDLE THROTTLE PLATE ADJUSTMENT SCREW

CHOKE CAM ADJUSTING SCREW FOR THROTTLE PLATE POSITION FOR CHOKING

IDLE ADJUSTMENT STOP

INLET SCREEN

THROTTLE LEVER

DRAIN PLUG

FUEL INLET

The early Ford carburetor (Detroit lubricator) was the very essence of simplicity. A single adjustment needle inserted down the single barrelled throat came close to offering a smooth idle condition. The single inlet fed all eight inlet valves.

Two water pumps were installed, one in each head. Unfortunately, the choice of location left something to be desired since the pumps were in the position of attempting to draw the heated water through the block and heads rather than working to push the relatively cooler water through as they would have been had they been mounted in the inlet end of the system. This condition, once having been accepted by Ford, prevailed until 1937 when they were moved to the block. These were the early "high-necked" water pumps; far more elaborate than later models.

The cast aluminum intake manifold (cataloged as a valve chamber cover) had a locking nut for the post-mounted generator, and here displays the high rise of the carburetor mount. The fitting, ahead and to the left of the oil filler hole, is the manifold vacuum attachment point for the windshield wiper.

View of the early Ford V-8 intake manifold with accessories mounted. Note difference in Air Cleaner from that shown in view on page 35. Either style would have been correct. Generator was three brush type with a cut-out to prevent discharge of battery through generator. Oil filler cap was simple in style.

Only one horn was installed on the 1932 V-8. This was originally a Sparks-Withington horn, later Sparton was furnished.

1932 Type 40 four passenger DeLuxe Roadster: *Mr. Carl Burnett, San Diego, California*

Hubcaps were rustless (stainless) steel, highly polished with the background of the V-8 done in Ford Blue. Tires are 5:25 x 18, an inch smaller in diameter than those of Model A, provided a more cushioned ride. Adding to the appearance, the wheel mounting lugs are concealed by the hub caps. Wheels were one piece, steel spoke, welded with drop-center rim and easily identified by the geometric beauty of the 32 spokes.

Rear curtain should be raised for increased
ventilation. Size of glass in curtain was 6″ x 19¹¹⁄₁₆″. Glass
was held in a chromed frame,
although inside half of frame was painted.

This view of rear-mounted spare wheel
illustrates what must have been an embarrassing
oversight. Aligning the wheel-mounting holes
with the lugs on the carrier produces the
effect shown here; the tire valve stem is found to
be off to one side! This condition
was corrected in '33 models.

The outside rear view mirror, obvious in
this view, was a DeLuxe feature. Standard
models were equipped with an inside mirror
only, and DeLuxe Roadsters were
furnished with only the outside one.
CLARA was selected for license in honor of
Mrs. Henry Ford.

The four cylinder Model B shared the same bodies as the Model V-8. The only external changes made to mark the four cylinder line were the deletion of the V-8 insignia (as shown) and the substitution of hub caps bearing the Ford script rather than V-8 adornment.

Cowl lights, provided on the DeLuxe models, were employed as parking lamps. Standard models employed two bulb-holders in the headlamp reflectors and parking lamps were then installed in the headlamp. A dual filament bulb in the tail lamp provided stop and tail lamp functions. Note that windshield could be folded flat.

Stainless steel brackets were employed to rest the top assembly and provided handholds for passengers in the rumble seat. Note the unusual pair of supplementary rubber bumpers provided to hold the rear window frames off the rear deck.

Large dual headlamps, 10 inches in diameter, and the centered V-8 were marks of the 1932 Ford. Headlamps, light cowl lights, were chrome plated and polished rustless steel.

The inviting DeLuxe rumble seat was upholstered in artificial leather, cobra drab in color. Standard roadsters offered an optional rumble at extra cost.

Back of rumble seat was only 22 inches wide, although the seat itself measured 37 inches. Floor covering was a rubber mat in standards, but the DeLuxe was carpeted.

Snaps, installed along the lower edges, made the removal of the entire top an easy matter. Position of striping is considered to be authentic.

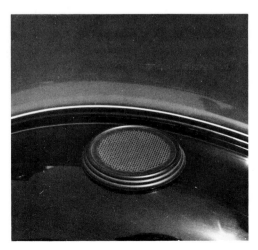

Rubber step mounted on crown of fender aided entry into rumble seat.

Windwings were adjustable and could be folded flat against windshield, which in turn could be lowered flat against the cowl.

Large front seat assembly (45 inches) was trimmed in genuine leather of copra drab. Standard Roadster was upholstered in artificial leather in two tone black/brown. Only the two main uprights of the top assembly were chrome plated. The balance of steel parts were painted, as was the inside rear window frame.

Formed receptacles in door sill allowed for the insertion of forged steel rods to support side curtains. Note beautiful handles employed on open cars.

Instrument panel includes knobs for throttle (left), choke (lower center), dash light (right) Ammeter on left, fuel gauge on right, and speedometer in center. Below instrument panel appears handle for cowl ventilator, new this year. Instrument cluster was engine-turned panel mounted on curved extender brackets protruding from the firewall. Oval slot in dashboard exposes panel but provides no point of attachment. Dashboard could be removed and instrument panel remains securely in place.

Wide doors contain utility pockets. Door-opening levers protrude through plated escutheon plates.

Accessory tire cover was painted black. Original style incorporated a chromed outer ring for additional dress-up effect on all DeLuxe models. This tire cover had no face plate covering wheel.

The top was made of canvas-like cloth, trimmed in leatherette. Exposed portions of wooden bows were formed, polished and varnished. The top folds flat against stands.

Rear view of DeLuxe Roadster with rumble seat. Right hand tail light should actually be a step plate (left), and not a light. The accessory right hand tail lamp is considered a good safety item, however, Ford did not offer a combination step plate and tail light bracket until 1933.

1932 Type 68 Cabriolet: *Mr. Charles Siems, Pasadena, California*

Greatly resembling the Roadster, the Cabriolet had, in addition to a different windshield support structure, the convenience of roll-up windows. With the top down, windows retracted, and especially with rumble seat open (as shown), the car definitely had a sporty look.

Windshield posts of cabriolet were extensions of the body and not separate chromed units.

Canvas of roof follows the edge of windows. Compare with that of Roadster on page 38.

Relatively large rear window of Cabriolet was almost three inches wider and higher than that of Roadster!

The original spare wheel lock is shown. Hub cap matches those on wheels and does not contain lock. The band, placed around wheel and locked, provided security.

Upholstery of Cabriolet, a strictly DeLuxe model, was full leather, both in passenger compartment and in rumble seat. Floor was carpeted throughout.

1932 Type 35 five passenger DeLuxe Phaeton:
Mr. Pete Rich, Palo Alto, California

(Rather than the correct factory-issue
tan top, this car now has a black Standard top.)

1932 Phaeton is listed as a five passenger car, versus the Roadster's four.
Rear seat of Phaeton was 46 inches wide, against 37 for the Roadster.

Single horn,
distinctive bumper,
add up to '32 V-8.

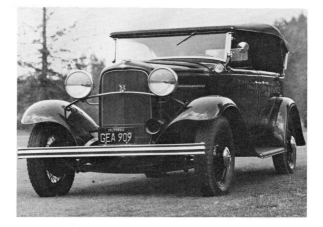

Single windshield wiper was vacuum operated, conected through a series of chromed tubes and rubber hose to the manifold fitting adjacent to the oil filler tube. Top was double texture rubber-interlined cloth. Standard Phaeton top was black rubber-like material and seats were of two-tone black/brown leatherette. DeLuxe models were upholstered in genuine leather (copra drab) with a tan interlined top. Cowl lights were standard equipment on DeLuxe models but the outside rear-view mirror, as shown, was an accessory.

The '32 gasoline tank, always painted black, was mounted between frame horns and protrudes from bottom of the body, as seen here. The frame itself extended beyond the tank and had a tubular rear cross member which sweeps upwards to provide rear mounting for spare wheel. When a luggage rack was used, this cross member was removed and replaced with the relatively straight rod on which the rack is mounted.

1932

Seats and backs were of genuine leather,
copra drab, colonial grain.
Standard Phaetons were similar, but for
the substitution of two-toned
black/brown artificial leather.

Floor covering was
carpeting; Standard
had rubber mats.

The foot accelerator was hinged
at the top and was therefore
more susceptible to jars and
bumps. After mastering it though,
it performed admirably.

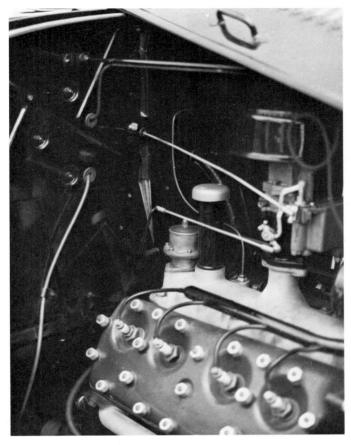

Characteristics of the early
'32 Ford V-8 include the fuel
pump mounted directly on the
intake manifold and the
single barrel Detroit
Lubricator carburetor with
early air filter.

The oil level dip-stick on the earliest models was a
bayonette type which gained access to the crankcase
via an opening in the block, located to the
rear on the right hand side. Note handle of dip-stick
protruding just behind the exhaust manifold, also the
high-necked water pumps.

An accessory, first offered in August of 1932, was the
water-temperature probe. Installed in the
radiator hose, the probe operated one half of a dual
water temperature/fuel level gauge and replaced the
single purpose fuel gauge on the instrument panel.

Detail of windwings reveals odd
shape of glass. Wings could be
folded against windshield and it,
in turn, folded flat on the hood.

Snaps were provided for the
attachment of side curtains;
receptacles in door sills
accommodate the curtain rods.

Chromed top assembly had an unusual '32
feature. Note the curved portion of the
rear metal arm extending below prop nut
and containing hole. A ⅜″ dowel,
located in the forward section of the top
frame, engaged this hole when top is
folded and provided a fairly good anchor.
Threaded top saddles were originally
furnished with the car but were generally
removed and stored when top was not
folded and their holes sealed
with rubber plugs.

1932 Type B-400 five passenger Convertible Sedan: *Mr. Sturl Sheff, Paramount, California*

1932

Six wheels and welled fenders
were optional accessories.
A rear-mounted spare was
normally supplied.

Spare wheels are mounted to a sturdy
bracket and protected by a locking-type
hub cap, (available after October of 1932).
Pivoting medalion exposed lock
(see lower photo). Note accessory
chromed 18″ beauty rings on wheels.

Radiator shell was
painted body color. The cap and
the flanged neck are die cast.

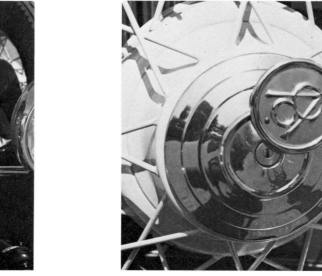

Windshield is plated and hinged
at top to open outwards.

Top, which ran in a channel at
top of the window frames, is held
in place by a series of snap
fasteners. Rear canvas gains
additional water protection from
the lipped flap.

Accessory rear view mirror mounts to windwings.
These, in turn, are an accessory offered by Ford.
Note that they are secured to the car
by means of expansible brackets not requiring
that there be holes drilled for mounts.

Sparton Model AF horn, motor-driven, was
replaced later in year by a vibrator type.
Only one horn was provided on the '32. Note
gentle outward curve of the headlamp lens.
The hood hold downs are T-head style.

Snap fasteners provide extra snug fit. Rear window flap does not open.

Rounded, almost hemispheric cowl lights, furnished as standard appointments on the Convertible Sedan are employed as parking lamps.

Closed car door handle of 1932-1934 series. Note the difference from that of open car, (see page 42).

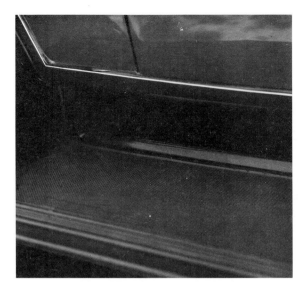

Frame of the '32 model served as an
important part of the body.
Running boards were bolted directly to
the frame, the lower portion of which
served as an appearance part of
the body itself.

Running boards were wide
and are mounted directly to
the frame. They are
of steel, rubber covered.

With the removal of the gas tank
to the rear of the body, a cowl
ventilator was added in 1932.
Operated by depressing a handle
under the dash, the opening
provided a flow of outside air
through the car.

An accessory trunk mounted
on the accessory rack smartens the
appearance of the rear.

1932

Louvered hood side panels allowed for additional engine cooling air to be expelled. Other ,earlier designs did not have upper edges of louvers in alignment with hood hinge line.

The right-hand tail lamp is an added safety and dress-up accessory.

Bumpers are chromium-plated, single bar type, and feature a design of some elaborate thought. The curve of the bumper at top and bottom was said to make it difficult to slide over or under another bumper.

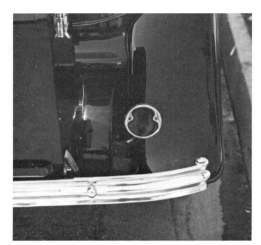

Hood opens to engine compartment by folding flat back on itself. No rests are provided in forward edge of body cowl.

Windshield, hinged at top, is opened outwards and clamped in place by ingenious design of tracked stay. Top, held in channel above windows provides an airtight seal.

Upholstery is Russet Brown leather with carpeting front and rear. Ash trays in rear were standard equipment on this model and other deluxe models. Safety glass was used for all windows on this model.

Light switch in center of steering wheel operates dual filament headlamps and parking lamps. Horn button is in center of switch. Steering wheel is not ornate, made of black hard rubber molded to a steel frame.

Accelerator was supplemented by a foot rest just to its right.

B400 is equipped with two bucket-style front seats. Passenger's side seat folds as shown in lower photos to allow for extremely easy access to the rear compartment.

Inside door panels are leather-trimmed and window riser and door handles are cast, plated and adorned with pressed steel, plated, escutheon plates.

1932 Model 160 — five passenger Standard Fordor Sedan,
cowl lamps, welled fenders, and trunk rack are accessories.

1932 Model 55 — five passenger DeLuxe Tudor Sedan

This DeLuxe Fordor Sedan has an accessory right rear tail lamp. The spare tire is rear-mounted as would be true of original.

Another view of rear-mounted accessory trunk and rack. Note absence of a tail lamp, (correct for 1932 models). Rear quarter window was fixed, does not open.

Standard windshield was painted. DeLuxe was plated and polished to provide more "dress-up". Windshield was mounted at a 10° angle to add to appearance and hinges were concealed in the upper headliner.

Note unusual style of the rear lamps.

Rear tail lamps were mounted by means of an integral bracket to the edges of the frame. This applied to both left side and also to accessory right side, when installed. A formed sheet metal shroud improved appearance of the frame horns.

The 1932 front fender was built without a skirt on the sides. Rather like Model A, they presented a narrow appearing edge behind wheel.

The welled fender was principally used on commercial cars which required rear-entry, but are highly sought after now due to their attractive appearance. Some few original cars were apparently sold with these welled fenders as optional equipment.

1932

1932 radio, manufactured by Grisby-Grunow was powered by a motor-generator. Radio control head was installed on steering column as shown here.

Motor-generator and electronics chassis were contained in sealed boxes which were inserted to their lip through holes cut in the floor pan forward of rear seat. This allowed boxes to drop under frame between the radius rods. Shown is a complete early radio including the two sealed containers and the control head.

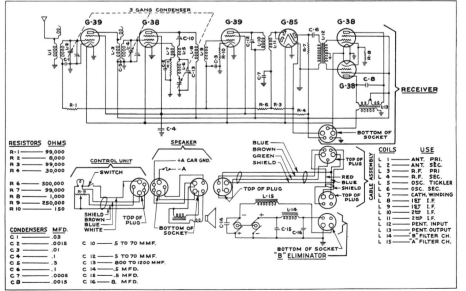

Schematic of the '32 motor-generator radio. Also available was a "fixed frequency" police version of same. No control head was furnished with this version, but frequency *was* adjustable at the chassis.

Ford B-18805 Auto Radio Receiver with Motor-Generator "B" Supply

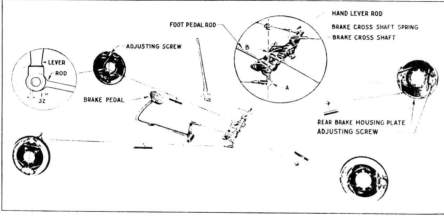

ADJUSTING SCREW

FOOT PEDAL ROD

HAND LEVER ROD
BRAKE CROSS SHAFT SPRING
BRAKE CROSS SHAFT

LEVER ROD

BRAKE PEDAL

REAR BRAKE HOUSING PLATE
ADJUSTING SCREW

1932 TO 1935 CAR BRAKE SYSTEM

The four wheel mechanical brake system originally furnished with the '32 was quite efficient and, until wear occurred in the clevis pins and holes became slots, they served to do an excellent job of stopping the car.

Original tool kit contained:

Lubricating gun
Jack and handle
Tire Iron
Tire pump
Combination crank
    and wheel wrench

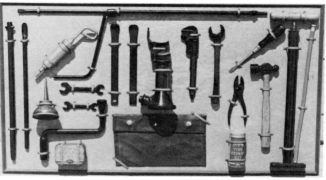

Pliers
Screw driver
Monkey wrench
Three open end wrenches
Artificial leather pouch

Also shown are accessory tire patch kit, oil can, hammer, and lamp bulb kit.

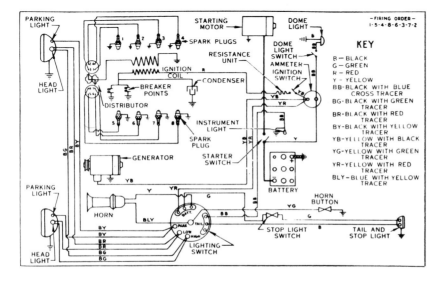

Wiring diagram of the '32. When cowl lamps were supplied, as on the DeLuxe models, a single bulb reflector was used in the headlamps and parking function was served by the cowl lamps. Otherwise, the reflectors were fitted with both the double filament headlamp bulb and also a single filament 3 candlepower parking lamp. Only one tail lamp was furnished although most cars do have accessory right rear lamps.

1932 Type 160 Fordor Sedan

1933 Type 730 Fordor Sedan

1933

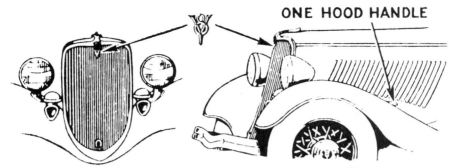

ONE HOOD HANDLE

Model "40," Ford Passenger Car

V-8 Engine   Approx. Weight, Std. Fordor, 2675 lbs.
112″ Wheelbase   Length, Bumper to Bumper, 175.9″
119.54″ Springbase   Width, overall, 67.4″

BODY TYPE	NAME	BODY TYPE	NAME
		PASSENGER	
700	Tudor Sedan (Standard)	730	Fordor Sedan (De Luxe)
700	Tudor Sedan (De Luxe)	740	Victoria
710	Roadster (Standard)	750	Phaeton (Standard)
710	Roadster (De Luxe)	750	Phaeton (De Luxe)
720	Coupe (Standard) (3 Window)	760	Cabriolet
720	Coupe (De Luxe) (3 Window)	770	Coupe (Standard) (5 Window)
730	Fordor Sedan (Standard)	770	Coupe (De Luxe) (5 Window)

Also, (commercially listed), Station Wagon, Type 860

65

By 1933, the generator had been equipped
with a four-bladed fan.
(see page 37 for early '32 style)

Ford's suspension, greatly improved by a *six inch increase* in wheelbase (to 112″)
was also helped in 1933 by a drastic change in the frame to include
a stiffening "X" member. To illustrate the flexibility of this new suspension,
Ford showed illustrations with front and rear opposite wheels propped
up on 12″ wooden blocks!

1933 saw the introduction of the locking *hubcap* for the *rear-mounted* spare wheel. While retaining the locking strap, the cap itself contained a keylock reached by rotating center escutcheon plates. (1932 similar caps were available for the side-mounted wheels, were not used on the rear) *see page 52.*

1933 Type 720 DeLuxe three window coupe: *Mr. Robert Kennedey, Whittier, California*

Rumble seat is opened by knob inside behind passenger's side of front seat. Rubber step plate on tail light and on fender aid entry.

Rumble seat passengers could converse with those inside through back window which could be completely lowered into body.

1933 Model 770 DeLuxe five window coupe: *Mr. Bob Hill, Sherwood, Oregon*

Available with either trunk or
rumble seat, rumble model would
have included step mounted
on right tail lamp.

Bodies were dropped slightly with the new wheels, now at 17 inches rather than 18 inch diameter. Deluxe models were furnished with two horns and cowl lamps. Hood was made to appear more streamlined by slanting the louvers.

The five window coupe featured a package shelf behind front seat. A T-headed knob, located below rear window on passenger's side enabled driver to lower rear window completely.

The trunk option is shown. Also available was a rumble seat option which was obtained by reversing the mounting of the deck lid with hinges affixed to bosses at the lower back. Lid was designed to be installed either way although once the handle was located and installed it was not then reversible.

Radiator grill has now been moved forward between fenders. Headlamps are more elliptical than '32.

Chromed windshield is hinged at the top and can be opened from the bottom. A crank-out mechanism with knob located at top center of dashboard offered access to this feature. Cabriolet model, however, had fixed windshield.

Rear quarter windows do not lower or rotate. Only the door- and rear windows may be lowered.

Cowl lamps on the DeLuxe models serve as parking lamps. Bumper guards are an accessory. Also, the crank hole cover is an accessory *(see page 73)*.

Interiors are done in mohair. Dual sunvisors are standard equipment.

Ring door pull is furnished to overcome the awkward location of inside door handle. Window risers on Standards were nickle plated; DeLuxe models had a mottled plastic spinner. Door panels were trimmed in mohair.

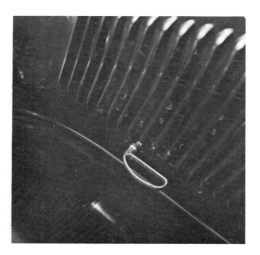

Single hood latch was nickle plated.

Rear-mounted spare was standard. Two tail lamps indicate a DeLuxe model.

No notch appears on cowl edge to support hood.

1933 Model 730 Fordor DeLuxe Sedan: *Mr. Kent Jaquith, Seattle, Washington*

Doors on same side are hinged at the rear. These front-opening doors became known as "suicide doors". This was due to danger which would result if opened while car was in motion. Nevertheless, in addition to providing the maximum access ease, they also offered the opportunity to allow passengers to enter or leave both the front and the rear seats at the same time.

Early 1933 style change included the addition of a skirt on the sides of the front fenders. Note contrast with the earlier style (insert).

A most rare accessory is the crank hole cover made of plated and polished steel.

1933

Radiator cap is relatively flat die casting.

Radiator grill has a definite, but slight, curve, as shown here. Headlamps are of polished plated rustless steel in a somewhat parabolic shape. Missing is V-8 escutcheon plate at top center.

Door handles on closed cars were made in rights and lefts. Same handle on both sides of the car for Fordors.

Another view of the door pull ring. Door handle is located at front edge of door.

1933 Model 700 DeLuxe Tudor Sedan: *Mr. Robert Flaner, Walnut Creek, California*

Car has accessory 16″ Kelsey wheels, first available in 1935.

Although somewhat boxy in appearance, the Tudor is nevertheless a most attractive automobile.

Front-opening doors allow for an easy egress. Right hand, or passenger's, seat tilts forward to allow entry to rear seat.

Curbside door, as on all closed models, includes a keylock for security. 1933 cowl light is more bullet-shaped than earlier 1932 style.

Tail lamp became more streamlined in appearance and mounted directly to the rear fender. Dual filament bulbs (3/21 cp) provide the tail- and stop-light functions. A switch mounted on the brake pedal assembly operates the stop light.

1933 Type 760 Cabriolet: *Mr. Donald Couch, Santa Rosa, California*

With rumble seat open, and especially with top down, this model was often mistaken for the Roadster. It, however, had roll-up windows and a windshield and dashboard treatment similar to closed cars. Unlike other closed cars, the windshield does not open. The handle employed to open the rumble seat was located *inside*, behind passenger on back of package shelf (rumble seat handle on Roadsters was located outside on the lid). Rear window curtain could be lowered if desired. Right hand combination step plate and tail lamp bracket was new this year.

1933

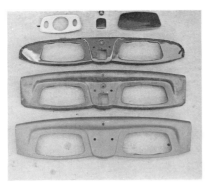

At top left is the instrument custer of the 1933 model. On the right at top is the glove box door (often replaced with a radio), and in the center the cigar lighter and ashtray inserts.

The upper 1933 dashboard was that for the Roadster and the Phaeton. Note difference in shape from center board which served the balance of the passenger cars (except Cabriolet which lacks windshield crank-out mechanism hole). As an interesting additional comparison, also shown (lower), is a commercial vehicle dashboard which lacks lighter and ashtray.

An interesting accessory gauge was this dual insert which offered a combined water temperature-fuel level gauge in place of single fuel level gauge.

Another interesting accessory gauge was this combination oil pressure (simply ON or OFF) plus ammeter, which could be substituted for the factory-issue ammeter.

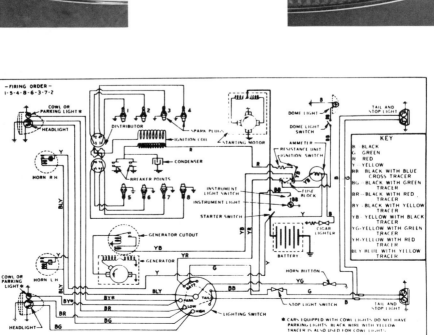

Wiring diagram of the 1933 DeLuxe Ford V-8

View of accessory rear-mounted trunk illustrates careful match of contours to rear of body and ingenious arrangement of gas tank filler. Trunk was furnished with necessary rear extensions for bumper and spare tire. Contrast with similar item on page 93 for later style.

Classic beauty of the 1933 front profile was heightened by accessory 17″ beauty rings.

The 1933 hubcaps were more elaborate than the later '34 style (right) and bore a sharply detailed, embossed V-8 with two discs or rings surrounding it.

1934

TWO HOOD HANDLES

Model "40," Ford Passenger Car

V-8 Engine   Approx. Weight, Std. Fordor, 2675 lbs.
112″ Wheelbase   Length, Bumper to Bumper, 175.9″
119.54″ Springbase   Width, overall, 67.4″

Most distinguishing mark of the 1934 hood was the two-handled locking arrangement. Compare with one-handle hood on page 71.

5:50 x 17 tires in wide whitewall. Chromed beauty rings were accessories.

A major change in '34 dashboard (lower) is that the instruments were mounted directly to the dashboard. The inserted instrument cluster used in 1933 (upper board) was eliminated.

BODY TYPE	NAME	BODY TYPE	NAME
	PASSENGER		
700	Tudor Sedan (Standard)	730	Fordor Sedan (De Luxe)
700	Tudor Sedan (De Luxe)	740	Victoria
710	Roadster (De Luxe)	750	Phaeton (De Luxe)
720	Coupe (Standard) (3 Window)	760	Cabriolet
720	Coupe (De Luxe) (3 Window)	770	Coupe (Standard) (5 Window)
730	Fordor Sedan (Standard)	770	Coupe (De Luxe) (5 Window)

Also, Station Wagon (listed as commercial) Type 860

1934 grill received wider chrome frame became more pointed, and lost the concave indentation of the 1933 grill.

Shown for comparison is the 1933 grill.

On, or about, January 1st, 1934, a change was made in the method of mounting the fuel pump. Formerly mounted on a horizontal surface, a pump was now mounted on a vertical surface, as shown. Shortly, a change in the manifolds deleted the earlier oil-filler tube hole entirely.

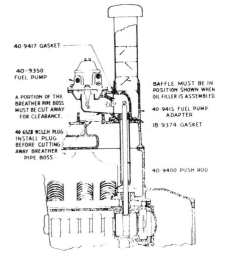

40-9417 GASKET

40-9350 FUEL PUMP

A PORTION OF THE BREATHER PIPE BOSS MUST BE CUT AWAY FOR CLEARANCE.

40-652B WELCH PLUG INSTALL PLUG BEFORE CUTTING AWAY BREATHER PIPE BOSS

BAFFLE MUST BE IN POSITION SHOWN WHEN OIL FILLER IS ASSEMBLED.

40-9415 FUEL PUMP ADAPTER

18-9374 GASKET

40-9400 PUSH ROD

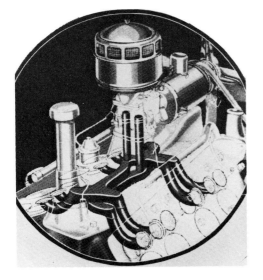

Manifold was changed to incorporate a dual-barrelled carburetor. Two discrete banks of four each inlet valves were coupled to each of the two sections of the manifold. Vacuum equalizing interconnections were made at the distributor automatic advance and the windshield wiper inlet in order to provide the smooth idle of an eight cylinder engine.

1934 Type 760 Cabriolet: *Mr. Gene Valdes, Downey, California*

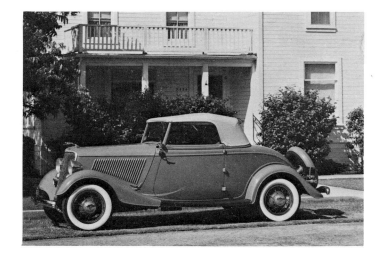

1934

Rear view mirror is an accessory. The cowl lights appeared for the last time this year.

Unlike the roadster with its chromed windshield supports, the windshield of the cabriolet is supported in a manner similar to that of the closed cars. Windshield did not open on cabriolet.

Two latching handles engaged brackets riveted to the sides of the cowl and to the inside edge of fender/frame.

DeLuxe models were equipped with two horns, Standard models had only one horn.

Accessory radiator cap displays slender form of traditional Ford greyhound.

1933 Greyhound is
shown for comparison.

The radiator's "V-8" was backed by triangular
shield. Note difference from 1933 style shown
on page 65.

Cowl lamps, same type as 1933, appeared for the
last time in 1934. Design of door handles required
left and right styles. Keylock was supplied on the
right hand or curbside front doors only.

1934

17″ chromed beauty
rings were
rare accessory.

The comfortable rumble seat, upholstered
in artificial leather provided additional
seating for two adults or three children.

Rubber step pad installed on
fender top.

Right rear tail lamp on rumble
seat models included this rubber
step plate, first introduced
in 1933.

Tool compartment is located in
right side panel of rumble seat.

Cabriolet had roll-down windows similar to other closed cars.

Top was of interlined canvas, and design allowed for a fairly airtight seal.

Front passenger compartment was upholstered in wool bedford cord. Seat and seat back were fully pleated. The door panels were lined and trimmed with the same cloth.

Operating handle for the rumble seat is located behind passenger side of front seat.

Top frame assembly was combination of chromed strap steel and wooden bows. Folding mechanism permitted top to be lowered into well behind the seat.

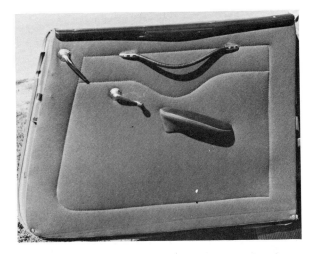

Door is now equipped with leather strap door loop rather than the metal ring shown on page 71. Later in 1934, the inside door handle was moved backwards, to center of the door, and the loop was eliminated.

1934

'34 engine compartment. 21 stud heads, dual barrel carburetor, and clean lines of cowl section.

Hood edge is now kept in place by the notch in the leading edge of the cowl.

Hood latching handles were formed from rod or wire and painted body color. They were no longer polished and plated castings.

The two-handled hood, a mark of the 1934 V-8.

1934 Model 710 DeLuxe Roadster: *Mr. Samuel Merrell, Portland, Oregon*

Spare tire, rear mounted, was protected by two-piece metal cover painted body color and with a chrome ring. The locking hub cap, with lock concealed under rotating Ford script plate, was hinged on a protective strap.

1934 Model 750 DeLuxe Phaeton: *Mr. Wallace Knute, Del Mar, California*

Narrow rear window (3^{15}⁄$_{16}$ by 23¾) is installed fairly high in back curtain. This allowed for best rear vision through rear view mirror.

Rear window is enclosed by a chrome plated frame. Two-piece frame bolts through the canvas curtain, inside half of the frame was painted.

Front view resembles other soft top models. Fog lamps were an accessory.

Unlike the 1932 Phaeton, the 1934 model had doors opening from the front and the rear.

Single chromed windshield wiper motor was vacuum-fed from manifold through series of rubber hoses and chromed steel tube affixed to left windshield support.

Interior of DeLuxe Phaeton was all leather. For the first time, Standard Phaeton was not offered in 1934.

A distinct ridge was embossed in the rim of the cowl. The purpose was questionable since windshield rubber flap did not coincide. Rear view mirror attached to windwing was an accessory.

Rear body lines were eased. Compare with photo of similar '32 model on page 47.

Rear-mounted spare tire is equipped with metal cover. Bumper guards were accessories.

Ford script escutcheon plate rotates to reveal keylock.

A very rare accessory was the '33/'34 rear-mounted trunk. Manufactured by Potter Manufacturing Company of Jackson, Michigan. The kit included a set of extenders under the trunk to mount the bumpers to the rear. Contours of forward face of trunk matches back of body exactly. The trunk was secured both to the extenders beneath it and also to body. Spare-tire carrier was affixed to rear of trunk.

Design of doors allowed for easy entry to both compartments at the same time, but added structural problems to the center post which had to be secured to the seat frame for support.

Unique hinge design. Used only in 1933 and 1934, it contrasted sharply with more common single-door style (insert).

The beautiful door handles, while different from front to back, actually required only two *pairs*. The opposite sides of the car used the same handles, reversed front to back. Snaps were provided for side curtains.

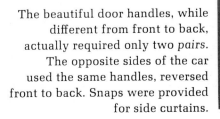

Accessory bumper guards have
characteristic "flattened" look.
Single line marks '33/'34 bumper.

Fender with skirt flows
beautifully with other lines.

Taillamp was affixed
directly to the fender by
an integral bracket.

With cowl ventilator open, a
refreshing flow of air prevailed.
This was the last year for the
beautiful cowl lamps.

Gasoline tank filler spout
protrudes through rear shroud.

1934 Model 730 Standard Fordor Sedan: *Mr. Sturl Steff, Paramount, California*

Only one horn was furnished
with the Standard Sedan.

Standard models did not have cowl
lamps. Parking lamps were obtained by
the installation of a separate 3 cp bulb
in a second receptacle in the headlamps.

Windshield frame of the Standard model was painted black. DeLuxe models were chromed.

An improved ventilation system was introduced on the 1934 sedans. By correctly turning the window regulator, the glass was caused to slide *backwards* to allow the indicated opening.

Illustrating the false frame provided as a receptacle for the window glass when opening, as above. Note difference from the similar location on the 1933 cars (above).

The inside door handle was moved to a more convenient position. This eliminated the need for the ring pulls, as provided in 1933.

Door panels were trimmed in matching mohair upholstery.

Dome lamp was chromed frame around frosted glass.

Rear quarter windows were provided with a T handle, which when rotated caused the glass to drop. Note also the arm rests in the rear seat.

A rear window shade was provided which hung from a roller mounted above the window. Eyes affixed to the pull rod on strings were installed on either side to prevent flapping.

Only one horn was provided on the Standard. The bell portion was not painted.

Other than the appearance of the single horn, there is no discernible evidence that this is not a DeLuxe model.

Storage battery was contained in a well under feet of the driver where it remained until the 1937 model. However, the fore and aft orientation was changed to side-to-side in 1935.

Water pumps have a lower neck than earlier style, but provide no temperature probe fittings.

Single tail lamp was provided on the Standard model.

1934 Model 740 Victoria: *Mr. Charley Bennett, Long Beach, California*

Extending rear quarter windows by 4″, over the sloping bustle back of the '34 Victoria now concealed the first of the internal luggage compartments ('33 Victoria did not have this feature). The gas filler cap and tube were located in the body of this model.

The entire rear panel could swing out. The control handle was located just under the back window on the inside right side of the car. Rear-mounted spare tire moved out with the bustle panel.

Collapsible canvas bellows protected items from falling out when trunk was opened. A metal framed canvas boot was furnished with the car and could be snapped into place to provide a cover for travel with the compartment open. The rear windows could be lowered, but the back window was fixed.

Rear quarter of 1932 Victoria, shown for comparison.

Victoria's passenger seat folded, up to mid 1934, and slid forward to offer additional entry space.

Early '34 passenger seat in normal position. Note the location of coin on carpet.

When folded back, the entire seat moves forward. Note the movement in relation to coin. This feature was discontinued during 1934.

The rear passenger compartment is spacious and does not indicate the existence of a luggage compartment. The back window had a pull-down window shade and ash trays were provided on both sides.

Introduced during 1934, the later style had a more 'up-to-date' front seat. Gone were the individual bucket-type seats of the earlier style, and the forward-moving seat. It was replaced by a seat assembly which tipped up and out of the way for entering passengers. Note the relocation of the door handle at the center of the front door.

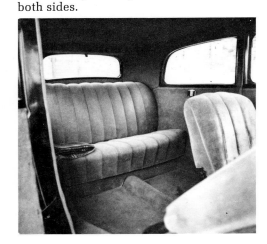

Radiator cap for the '34 was higher than the '33 and marked one difference between the cars. This was the last functional external radiator cap. The radiator filler was relocated under the hood in 1935.

1933 radiator cap was flatter and the grill frame was narrower.

Rarer still, this accessory greyhound radiator cap, which also contains a temperature gauge!

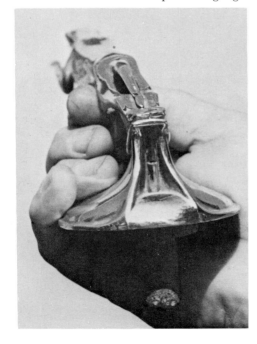

The original and highly prized Ford greyhound accessory radiator cap. This was the last year in which this cap actually served other than a decorative purpose until 1937.

1934 Type 700 DeLuxe Tudor Sedan: *Mr. Robert Stewart, San Diego, California*

Chromed windshield frame,
dual horns with chromed tops
and bells, and cowl lamps
marked this as the DeLuxe
model.

Headlamps on models with cowl lamps
contained only one dual filament
(32/32 cp) bulb. The parking lamp
function was supplied by the cowl lamp.

Tudor Sedan, in this view, bears
a strong resemblance to the
Victoria model, however, the rear
quarter windows are
six inches longer!

The back window was the same
size in both Tudor and Victoria.

Backs of bucket-type front seats folded forward to allow easy entry to the rear seat.

Dashboard included a "package compartment" and, as shown, a Ford center control radio. The knob above the radio head cranks out the lower edge of the windshield. Right-hand instrument was the original single purpose gasoline gauge.

Original upholstery, now protected by clear plastic, was made of bedford cord. The carpet was woolen in the rear with a rubber mat in front. The back of the front seat tilted and the passenger seat pivoted as a unit.

The back window could not be lowered and was equipped with a pull-down window shade.

"Toggles" (hand assists) were swiveled from the doorpost. Ash trays were furnished on each side with arm rests in the back seat only. The window trim and dashboard were woodgrained.

The original stripe, Tacoma Cream, to match the wheels, on an original paint job. The Triple Stripe was included on the 1933 - 1934 models only and then discontinued.

1934 Type 860 Station Wagon: *Mr. Frank Hoyt, Vista, California*

In an attempt to overcome the exhaust fumes, Southern California Edison, the original owner, modified the exhaust pipe by adding a riser to extend above roof line. Also added was a trailer hitch.

Five wheels, with the spare mounted on the right side, characterized the Station Wagon.

The windshield opened by means of crank mechanism located in upper dash center. A wide headliner above windshield concealed the wiper motor.

Original windwing. Note that these actually screw into the wooden body.

High mounting of spare tire presented an awkward appearance, however, it was quite practical. Door handles shown are of the closed car style, rather than the more ornate open car style.

1934 Type 770 DeLuxe 5 window Coupe: *Mr. Kendall Tucker, Torrance, California*

The trunk handle is stainless, and installed so that it points forward when in a latched position.

With the trunk lid open, note the awkward position of rear-mounted spare. Storage space, however, was quite adequate.

The T-headed knob at top center of dashboard cranks lower edge of windshield open (as shown). Left hand instrument is ammeter, center is speedometer, and on right, fuel level gauge. Ignition switch is OFF in "up" position, lights are controlled by the ring switch around the horn button.

1934

Cowl lamps appeared for last
time in 1934. There was no outside door lock on the drivers side.

The keylock for car was
located on the right side only.

The inside of the right front door shows
an accessory armrest. Note the inside
door lock which blocks handle from
outside opening. The 1934 inside door
handle was relocated to a more
convenient position than in the '33 models.

Interior upholstery is duplicate
of original stripe. The material
is Bedford Cord however,
original material was an all-wool
cloth, much like serge
in appearance.

Although the rear quarter windows were fixed, the back window could be lowered by turning the knob located below window and behind passengers side of front seat. The location made it possible for the driver to reach.

Entire seat-frame assembly could be moved forward by the releasing latching mechanism. The handle was located below the front of seat.

The back window had a roller window shade. Two strings were provided to keep the ends of the roller from flapping. Note, however, that the strings are missing in this photo.

The rear window could be lowered "all the way" into a wooden framework behind seat.

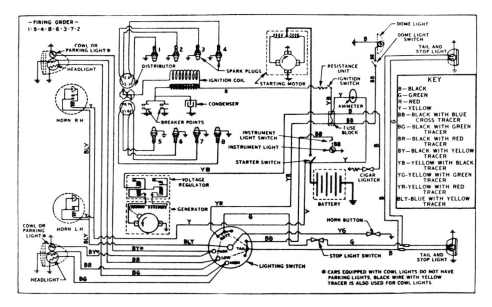

Wiring diagram for 1934 Ford Standard.

On DeLuxe cars, or Standards that were equipped with cowl lamps as an accessory, the parking light in the headlamp reflector was eliminated. Probably as a result of general conversion to the attractive cowl lamps, the wiring diagram makes clear reference to the matter.

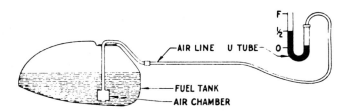

Schematic diagram of
hydrostatic fuel gauge system.

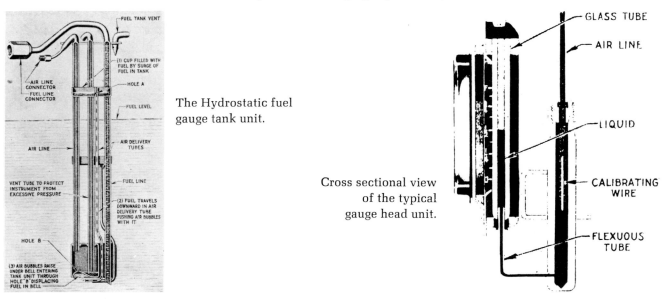

The Hydrostatic fuel
gauge tank unit.

Cross sectional view
of the typical
gauge head unit.

1934 Type 750 DeLuxe Phaeton

1932 Type 35 DeLuxe Phaeton

1935

Model "48," Ford Passenger Car

V-8 Engine   Approx. Weight, Std. Fordor, 2849 lbs.
112″ Wheelbase   Length, Bumper to Bumper, 182.75″
123.13″ Springbase   Width, overall, 69.5″

BODY TYPE	NAME	BODY TYPE	NAME
	PASSENGER		
700	Tudor Sedan (Standard)	730	Fordor Sedan (Touring)
700	Tudor Sedan (De Luxe)	740	Convertible Sedan
700	Tudor Sedan (Touring)	750	Phaeton
710	Roadster	760	Cabriolet
720	Coupe (3 Window)		
730	Fordor Sedan (Standard)	770	Coupe (Standard) (5 Window)
730	Fordor Sedan (De Luxe)	770	Coupe (De Luxe) (5 Window)

Also, Station Wagon (listed commercially) Type 790

This was the last year for the exposed horn. The horns appearance on this car is clearly vestigal.

Bodies underwent a major redesigning in 1935. The leading edge of the radiator was moved (along with the engine) almost eight inches forward! Compare the position with similar photo of 1934 style, shown below. Wheels were now 16″ diameter, lowering the car an additional half-inch.

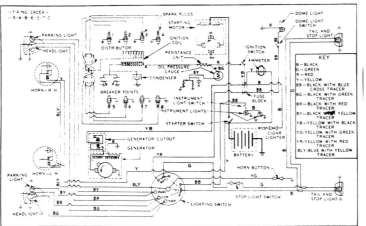

Wiring Diagram 1935 Ford V-8.

A highly desirable accessory rack was the rear-mounted luggage rack. It was designed to hold its load behind the rear mounted spare tire assembly and yet fold well out of the way when not in use.

1935

1935 brought a number of changes, among them a significant change in the engine block casting to provide a "flow-through" crankcase ventilation. Air was directed by means of the scoop-shaped oil filler cap, through the crankcase, up into the valve chamber past a series of baffles, and then exhausted down through a vent at the forward right surface of the oil pan. Domed pistons were introduced and a cast alloy steel crank was used in place of the earlier forged crank. Also, the block was modified to allow for the insertion of an oil pressure probe at left rear.

A major change in 1935 was the addition of a set of counterweights to the clutch which acted centrifugally to increase pressure on clutch. Increased speed, thereby, reduced a tendency to slip. This feature has been retained in all models since 1935.

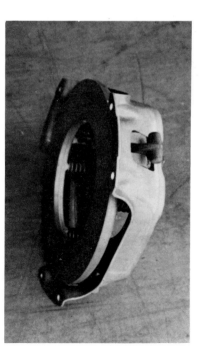

Although most other manufacturers had already introduced hydraulic brakes, Ford retained a mechanical braking system. The four wheel brakes were applied through a series of levers and crankarms, and when properly adjusted, did an excellent job of stopping the car. Mechanics were cautioned to back off the adjustments of the front brakes slightly in order to prevent an overload on the front brakes.

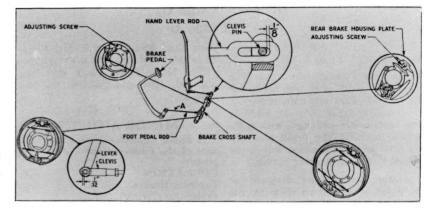

Water pump housing was modified to allow for the insertion of water temperature probe, now a standard dashboard instrument.

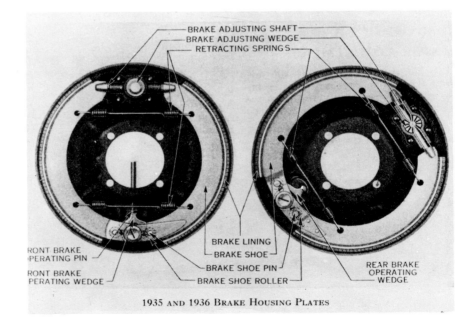

1935 AND 1936 BRAKE HOUSING PLATES

1935 Type 710 Roadster: Mr. Richard Palmer, Encino, California

The doors now open at the rear, a definite safety advantage.

Door handles in 1935 were straight and more austere than the gracefully curved earlier handles.

The lower right front fenders were one-piece assembly.

Wheels were reduced to 16 inch and tires were 6:00 x 16. This was the last year for the beautiful 32 spoke wire wheels by Ford.

Headlamps were now painted the body color, except for polished steel ring around lens. The glass lens itself was relatively flat and not domed.

The bumper, although similar to earlier models, was a double line trim rather than single. Bumper guards were more slender and not "flattened".

Beam adjustment on 1935 (and '36) lamps was made by loosening a locking nut below the fender and swiveling lamp in the desired direction.

1935

Greyhound now leaps from fixed position. The radiator cap was concealed under left side of the hood. The mascot was an accessory added to basic V-8 nose trim.

Windwings were held at the edge by two clamping type brackets. Stanchions contained raised bosses drilled and tapped to accept the threaded ends of clamps.

1934 style for comparison.

The rumble seat was artificial leather lined with a rubber floor mat. Construction of the upholstery is similar to original. Rubber step plate was provided on the right fender top for entering passengers.

Hub cap cover on wheel is '34 style (note wide flare of painted oval). Correct style for the 1935 model is shown.

Rumble handle was T-headed. Rear-mounted spare wheel had metal cover in a new size to accommodate 16″ wheels.

The horn is the same as the previous vibrator type, drawing about 15 amps when energized. It had a black-painted body with a chromed bell and cap.

The cowl ventilator followed the curve of hood to provide more symmetrical appearance.

The '35 front end seemed massive with a fairly flat grill and could be accentuated by accessory bumper guards.

Four chrome strips were employed to trim the louvers in the sides of the hood.

1935 Type 750 Phaeton: *Mr. Ollie Smith, El Cajon, California*

Right hand tail lamp (furnished on DeLuxe cars), was painted body color with a stainless steel polished trim. Fairing at forward end of lamp concealed two mounting bolts and a hole for wiring.

Back again this year is the top saddle. Leather lined and with a strap to hold the retracted top securely (to prevent chafing of the canvas), they screwed into right-and-left-handed castings secured in the wooden framework of the body.

Top, (tan canvas), trimmed with brown leatherette, was stretched over a collapsible framework of chromed steel and wooden bows (and front header). Rear bow had an eight inch radius and the forward bow had a six inch radius.

Factory standard trim of the 1935 V-8 Ford

Outside hinge-pin mounted mirror was an accessory. Note the fasteners on the leading edge of the windshield stanchions for the side curtains.

The rear mounted spare in metal tire cover with a locking hub cap.

1935 Type 740 Convertible Sedan: *Mr. Bill Bolger, Portland, Oregon*

Returning in 1935 was the Convertible
Sedan, last manufactured in 1932.
Now a four door convertible, the roll-up
windows and side posts gave passengers
a weathertight closed car, as well as
an extremely good looking open car.
Chrome trim strip at edge of running
board was standard equipment on the
Convertible Sedan and DeLuxe Touring
Sedans.

Rear body lines were similar to
the Phaeton. With a rear-mounted
spare and accessory luggage
rack, the car presents a racy
appearance.

The rear curtain could be lowered
to provide additional ventilation.

The banjo wheel was an accessory mark of
the DeLuxe line and frames the instrument
cluster and radio control head. The left-
hand dial is a combination oil pressure
and fuel level gauge. Instruments are
silver-faced with red trim. 1935 was the
last year that the hydrostatic fuel gauge
was available.

The Phaeton and Roadster
dashboards were narrow with a
tapered glove box door.

Ash tray, in this dash, to right of radio
head, was an optional installation.
The accessory clock in the glove box
door was also optional. Note that in the
Convertible Sedan and the Station Wagon
(as in open cars) there was no windshield
crank-out mechanism. Dual-indicating
electric oil pressure gauge (with
hydrostatic fuel gauge) was introduced
in 1935. See page 132 for operating diagram.

The closed car dashboard was more
massive. The glove box door was more
nearly rectangular. Station Wagon and
Convertible Sedan dashs were similar
but lacked a hole in the top center for the
crank-out windshield mechanism.

1935 Type 700 Tudor Touring Sedan: *Mr. Don Hawes, Albany, Oregon*

The header-bar radio, new that year, permitted the radio speaker to be installed overhead, between the sun visors. The installation helped rear seat passengers to hear the radio.

The 1935 Touring Sedan was distinguished by the addition of a rear-mounted integral trunk.

Although beautiful in appearance and modern in design, the integral trunk, offered for the first time, was actually somewhat inconvenient. With a narrow opening, and the spare in the way, access to the storage area was difficult.

Large rear window of the Tudor, as shown here, could be lowered. The trunk provided protected storage space for luggage. 1935 was the first year safety glass was used on all closed cars.

1936

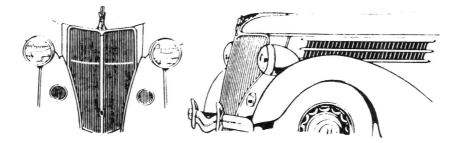

Model 68 Ford Passenger Car
8 cylinder (112″ wheelbase)

BODY TYPE	NAME	BODY TYPE	NAME
	PASSENGER		
700	Tudor Sedan (Standard)	730	Fordor Sedan Touring (Standard)
700	Tudor Sedan (De Luxe)	730	Fordor Sedan Touring (De Luxe)
700	Tudor Sedan Touring (Standard)	740	Convertible Sedan
700	Tudor Sedan Touring (De Luxe)	750	Phaeton
710	Roadster	760	Cabriolet
720	Coupe (3 Window)	760	Club Cabriolet
730	Fordor Sedan (Standard)	770	Coupe (Standard) (5 Window)
730	Fordor Sedan (De Luxe)	770	Coupe (De Luxe) (5 Window)

Also, Station Wagon (listed commercially) Type 790

Gone were the fancy wire wheels of earlier years. The solid steel wheels of 1936 were trimmed with a polished steel and the painted cover exposed only a small portion of the wheel itself. Tire size was 6:00 x 16.

130

High "wings" of the "V" were a hazard
and careless folding of the hood on either
side would break off the "ears".
As a result, very few have survived
to this day.

Greyhound accessory
was a prized "dress-
up" item.

REAR WHEEL BEARINGS

During 1936, rear wheel drums were modified
to permit the use of smaller bearing, plus a
hardened sleeve race. Later, smaller bearing hub
had pressed in hardened race.

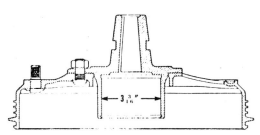

LARGE BEARING TYPE REAR HUB

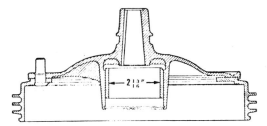

SMALL BEARING TYPE REAR HUB

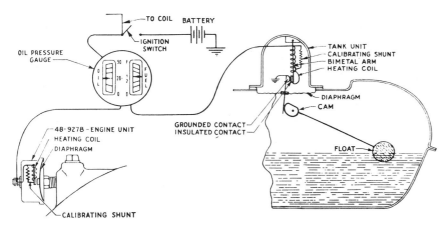

1936 brought a new sense of instrumentation. Oil pressure gauge and fuel gauge had been incorporated on left side of dashboard, in 1935, but new this year was electric fuel gauge. Both instruments were bi-metallic strips operated by a voltage divided resistor network.

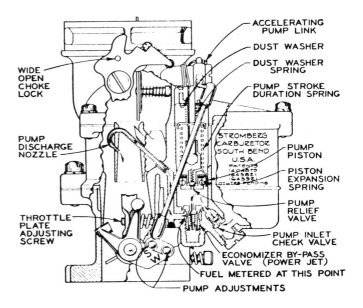

Stromberg 97 carburetor, introduced in April of this year, was an economical dual-throat carburetor with accelerating pump and idle adjustments.

Bumper guards were, of course, accessories. In 1934 they were fairly flat-faced but the 1935/36 style showed good design in that they were rounded and more slender.

Former President Franklin Delano Roosevelt. The photo was taken in 1937. Car is a 1936 Phaeton especially equipped with controls for his use. Note early door handles and special accessory wheelcovers.

1936 Type 740 Convertible Sedan: *Mr. Ollie Smith, El Cajon, California*

Accessory right-hand windshield wiper is "slaved" to the motor-driven wiper on driver's side. Horns are concealed behind dual grills in the fender inner panels. The fender was a two-piece assembly with chrome welting. Compare with similar view of '35 on page 120.

With windows up, the car is practically weather-tight.

Dual tail lamps are mounted
on trunk lid rather than fenders.

Trunk was hinged at the top and was
held closed with two latches.
There was no handle as such.

With trunk lid opened, spare tire,
is exposed below protective deck. Trunk
appears to have more storage space than
actually existed.

Early in the year (following style of 1935 model),
Convertible Sedans were manufactured with rear
section similar to the Phaeton. There was a
modest storage space behind the rear seat.
Integral trunk model was introduced in April
of 1936.

Tail lamps were rather stubby
and mounted, as shown, on the
trunk cover rather than on
the fender.

A unique rubber grommet
shielded filler neck. The locking
gasoline cap was an accessory.

A chromed two-piece frame
holds glass in the canvas top. Back
flap could be lowered for ventilation.

All four windows could be cranked down
into the doors. Robe rail was an
accessory item. This car has upholstery
similar to closed cars.

Body trim plate between windows was
removable. Two knurled screws held the
piece in place. With windows down
and this piece removed car resembled
the windowless Phaeton.

Car was carpeted front and rear. The windshield supporting frame was common with other closed cars, however, not with the Roadster nor Phaeton.

Uniquely executed V-8 adorns the trunk lid.

Window inside trim and dashboard were woodgrained. Position of handle in rear door was forward.

Pleats sewn into Bedford Cord seats were the typical style. Upholstery here is Bedford Cord, although a leather option was available. Top frame assembly was not interchangeable with Phaetons.

Front seat assembly was an imposing structure with back of front seat inserted into wide lip of supporting frame. Phaeton assembly differs.

Ignition switch Keylock is in OFF position. Late in 1936, and for all of 1937, this switch mechanism was reversed and OFF became the "down" position of lock.

Convertible Sedan (left) and Station Wagon (above) share unique dashboard. Note the absence of crank-out knob, as windshield in each is fixed. Both models had cowl ventilators though.

Likewise, these two cars share a unique windshield. Compare station wagon windshield (below) with "ordinary" closed car (right). Top was relatively flatter with sharper curves at each end.

1936 Type 790 Station Wagon: *Mr. Charley Bennett, Long Beach, California*

Rear-mounted spare tire cover and canvas
rear curtain marked the 1936 wagon.
No tail lamp appeared on the right side.

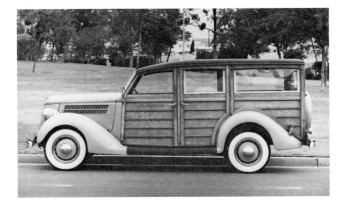

1936

Rectangular form of windshield differed from other models (except convertible sedan).

Only windshield and front doors were glassed. Roll-up windows in front doors had been introduced in 1935.

Canvas side curtains with clear inserts were provided.

Head lamps of '36 display wider chromed frame and domed lens. 1935 (insert) was flatter. Rear portion of headlamp was painted body color. 1936 was the last year for separate head lamps. DeLuxe horn grill covers were either cast, brass or stainless and plated; standards were steel, painted black. A protective gasket was inserted between the cover and fender.

Three chromed strips trim louvers of '36 hood. Six ply tires were standard on station wagon and four ply on all other models.

Heavy forged latching
mechanism held tail gate
in position.

With tail-gate lowered, rear-mounted
spare would have struck bumper guards,
hence, these were not used on the
station wagon rear.

Rear seat pivoted forward
to provide additional loading
space. Leather-sleeved chains
provided linkage for support.

Body rides on rear fenders.
Station wagons from 1935 to 1937
used the same rear fenders.

Long filler neck was used on the
station wagon. Locking cap was
an accessory.

Accessory 1936 clock face
matched the other instruments.
Glove box knob was standard on
DeLuxe models.

Wooden roof was covered with
impregnated canvas for weather protection. It extended forward to the body
section and behind the windshield a
single wiper motor was concealed.

Seating arrangement easily
accommodated up to seven passengers.
With side curtains raised into the
roof, it was fresh air all around!

Two bucket-type seats were not
identical, but were right and left handed
so that lines of seatback followed the
door sill. Side curtains pushed up into
storage tracks built into the roof.

Clean lines of the '36 front end were emphasized by concealment of the horns behind chromed (on DeLuxe) grills.

Rear doors opened forward for best access.

Inside door handle of the station wagon was unique. Note flowing lines.

Rear-mounted spare wheel was protected by a locking hubcap. Bumper was the same as 1935 and interchangeable from front to rear.

1936 Type 750 Phaeton: *Mr. Jack McNeil, Buena Park, California*

Grill, originally chromed, has been painted black.

A top boot, not installed in this photo, added to the elegance of this open car. The sweep of the front fender is far less graceful than that of '35 (page 124).

When folded back, the top was captured in the saddle with a leather strap to prevent chafing of the canvas. A boot was supplied which could have been snapped to fasteners installed on the narrow shelf behind the rear seat.

"Straight" type door handles, common with '35, were replaced later in the year with "curved" style like the '37 models.

Windwing brackets now fit top and bottom, holding glass more securely. (Contrast with '35 style on page 125.) A change was made in the windshield stanchions, eliminating the bosses necessary with the 35 style windwings and adding the lower one required with this design.

Leather seats and leatherette door panels mark the '36 Phaeton. Cowl had only a minor lip, (unlike the distinct roll found on the '33-'34 style body), and it coincided with the lower rubber weatherseal of the windshield in the closed position.

1936 accessory clock mirror shows face to be similar to trim of other instruments (see bottom picture).

Center-control radio was flanked by (upper) instrument panel light switch (left) and cigar lighter (right), and lower, throttle (left) and choke (right).

Glove box door had a distinctive plastic knob. Also, available was a keylock. Brake handle extension and Southwind gasoline heater were accessories.

Accessory "Banjo" steering wheel for 1935-1936, a most popular "dress-up" item, had straight steel spokes, chrome plated. Horn button bears familiar V-8, and light switch is quite flat, and disc-shaped.

Four ply 6:00 x 16 tires were standard in
1936, except on the Station Wagon (and other
commercial vehicles) where six ply tires
were used. Hup caps had an indented V-8
design and ring and the face was of
polished rustless steel.

1936 Type 710 Roadster: *Mr. Carl Burnett, San Diego, California*

Accessory spider hubcaps, covered the entire wheel, including spokes, with a chrome-plated, polished decorative cover.

Accessory windwing mirror was attached to the windwing with a clamp. Snap fasteners are for side curtains.

Accessory exhaust deflector helped to divert exhaust from soiling bumper. Rear window flap could be lowered.

1936

New in 1936 was the Club
Cabriolet with room for two
additional passengers seated
behind front seat. Contrast view
with that of Roadster,
previous page.

The oversized roof was a mark
of the Club Cabriolet, as is
evident in this view.

1936 Type 760 Club Cabriolet, with accessory spider wheelcovers:

Mr. Walter Schmeiser, Camby, Oregon

Windshield posts of Cabriolets
were built like closed cars, with
no separate chromed items, as on
Roadster and Phaeton.
The windshield did not open.

Integral trunk is hinged at the
top and offers reduced,
but adequate, storage space.

1936 Type 730 DeLuxe Fordor Touring Sedan: *Mr. Marlon Pulst, Kirkland, Washington*

Differing from the Fordor Sedan, the Touring Sedan incorporated an integral "hump-backed" trunk.

This was the last year for an external-mounted spare on sedans.

Rear quarter windows pivoted to open for ventilation on 1936 models. The 1935 Model windows did not pivot.

1932 Type B-400 Convertible Sedan

Mr. Sturl Sheff, Paramount, California

1932 Type 40 DeLuxe Roadster

Mr. Carl Burnett, San Diego, California

1935 Type 710 Roadster

Mr. Richard Palmer, Encino, California

1934 Type 750 Phaeton

Mr. Wallace Knute, Del Mar, California

1936 Type 750 Phaeton

Mr. Jack McNeil, Buena Park, California

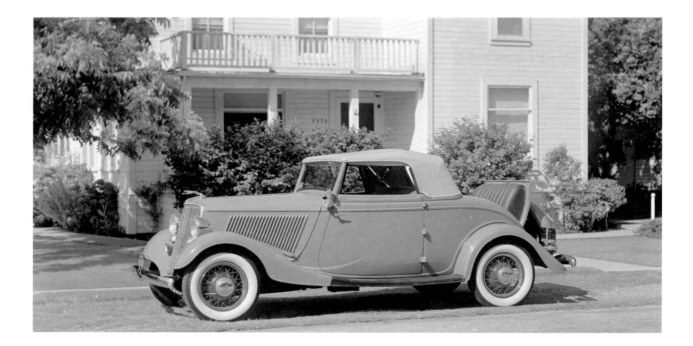

1934 Type 760 Cabriolet

Mr. Gene Valdes, Downey, California

1937 Type 750 Phaeton

Mr. Ollie Smith, La Mesa, California

1936 Type 790 Station Wagon

Mr. Charley Bennett, Long Beach, California

1940 Type 79-B DeLuxe Station Wagon

Mrs. Charles Leffingwell, Cardiff-by-the-Sea, California

1936 Type 740 Convertible Sedan

Mr. Ollie Smith, La Mesa, California

1939 Type 74 DeLuxe Convertible Fordor Sedan

Mr. Gordon Chamberlin, Granada Hills, California

1935 Type 750 Phaeton

Mr. Ollie Smith, La Mesa, California

1936 Ford, custom body by Jensen Motors, Ltd, West Bromwich, England

Mr. Warren Wyman, Rancho Santa Fe, California

1936 Type 700 Standard Tudor Sedan: *Mr. Fred Tweedie, Salem, Oregon*

Only one tail lamp was furnished on Standard
models. The "slant" back of this car identified it
as "Tudor Sedan", rather than "Tudor Touring
Sedan" which had integral trunk.

Black-painted radiator grill and horn
covers were additional marks of the
Standard model. Beauty rings on wheels
were a dress-up accessory.

1937 Type 700 DeLuxe Tudor Touring Sedan;
note obvious difference in rear body line from above car.

DeLuxe models had two tail lamps,
obvious in this view. The integral trunk
was hinged at top and latches
secured the cover.

Standard models were equipped
with only one tail lamp,
on the left. "Slant-black" model
had rear seat hinged and would
fold forward to provide limited
storage behind the seat.

When latches were unlocked, rear edge
of cover would swing clear of the rear
mounted spare and open to storage space.
Chrome ring trim of spare tire
cover is missing.

Clean lines of the back were uncluttered
and, in this view, may have been superior
to trunk models.

1936 Type 770 five-window coupe

1936 Type 720 three-window coupe

1936 Type 720 three-window Coupe: *Mr. Max Lee, Lebanon, Oregon*

With rumble seat, the car was a popular and sporty model. Trunk option provided a good-looking businessman's car. The three window coupe was only available in one version, a generally DeLuxe trimmed car. There was no standard model.

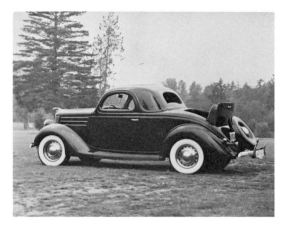

Prized Spider hubcaps and greyhound radiator mascot were desirable accessories.

Back window could be lowered by knob that was below the window, on right side behind passenger's seat.

For the last year roof panels were constructed with a water-proofed canvas-like material installed over a chicken-wire frame.

Rumble seat was opened by means of a T-headed handle located on lid. Leatherette upholstery and rubber mat were in the rumble. Bedford cord and carpet was in the front seat compartment.

Five window coupe appeared to be more spacious than three-window. The rear quarter windows did not open. A large package shelf appeared behind the front seat under back window.

1936 Type 770 DeLuxe five-window Coupe: *Mr. Jack Ramsey, Oregon City, Oregon*

Accessory Pines trim (see next page) were dress-up items shown to better advantage over black-painted radiator grill, normally a Standard feature.

Trunk, hinged at front and opened from bottom rear was a feature of the car, although a rumble seat option was available.

Back window was fixed and could not be opened. The exhaust deflector, like bumper guards, were accessories.

1936

Pines Trim was an accessory becoming increasingly rare. Generally installed over black-painted grill for effect, and with "bullnose" or smooth hood ornament, the installation of the ten piece set greatly changed the appearance of the Ford.

Together with the Spider hubcaps, the Pines Trim set was used to "upgrade" the appearance of the car. Although distinctive in appearance, it was obvious that these improvements added nothing to safety, economy, or performance.

This unusual dress-up accessory was extremely rare. Adding only to appearance, the effect, heightened by the special "V-8", was remarkable.

1936 Standard spare
wheel cover differed
from that supplied with
DeLuxe models (below).

Rear-mounted spare wheel was protected by a keylock set in the hub of cover. Although cap could be easily opened, the rear dish of the two-piece tire cover set was almost impossible to remove without using a key to retract three locking plungers engaged in the wheel hub. 1936 was last year for an exposed spare tire.

Although not strictly a "pre-war Ford V-8", this car is *almost* that! One of three '36 Ford chassis modified by Jensen Motors, Ltd., in West Bromwich, England, by the addition of a specially-constructed aluminum sports body. It survives today as a classic example of coachbuilding. Production versions of the Jensen also employed Ford's V-8 engine and running gear, but these three were the only ones to also employ a good part of the Ford's production sheet metal.

1936 Ford with special Jensen Motors body: *Mr. Warren Wyman, Rancho Santa Fe, California*

Distinctive sports-car styling is predominantly apparent.

Sweep of chrome trim and lines of running board minimize the appearance of built-in turn signals.

Headlamps, windshield, and parking lights were just a few of the distinctive items on this car.

Extra long hood was lowered and carburetor could not accommodate an air cleaner.

Specially designed windshield support stanchions blended with the body.

Parking lamps on fenders and special bowl-shaped chromed headlamps add to the unique appearance.

A very comfortable bench seat and
two deep bucket seats accommodated
four people.

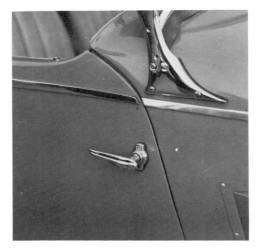

Ford running boards were
replaced with chrome-ribbed
steel boards with a long sweep.

Even door handles were unique.
However, like the lights, were
probably taken from Jensen's standard
production lines.

Original steering wheel was a
four-spoked banjo. Dashboard
was made of wood panel insert
in steel shell.

Seat was moved well to the
rear, requiring special mechanism
to permit shifter lever to
operate transmission, hence the
long "tunnel".

Dual cowl side
vents were provided.

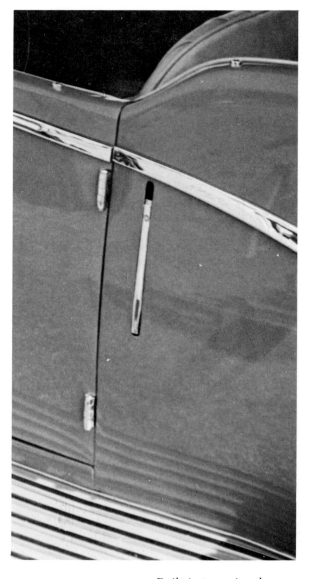

Built-in turn signals were
arms concealed in the body.
They 'popped-out' to display
lighted tip.

Distinct notch in rear body panel allowed top, when folded, to lie in an almost horizontal position.

Two handles secured deck lid. Inside storage was adequate, but not superb.

The hood latch handles, both at front and rear of hood, were chromed.

The spare tire was carried in a standard metal cover. The tail lamp was mounted on the license bracket secured to tire cover. Bumpers and guards were standard '36 style.

1937

The hood ornament served a useful function; turning it released the latch.

MODEL 78 FORD Passenger Car, 8 cylinder 85 HP Engine (112" wheelbase)
MODEL 74 FORD Passenger Car, 8 cylinder 60 HP engine (112" wheelbase)

BODY TYPE	NAME	BODY TYPE	NAME
PASSENGER			
700-A	Tudor Sedan (Standard)	730-C	Fordor Sedan (Standard Touring)
700-B	Tudor Sedan (De Luxe)	730-D	Fordor Sedan (De Luxe Touring)
700-C	Tudor Sedan (Standard Touring)	740	Convertible Sedan
700-D	Tudor Sedan (De Luxe Touring)	750	Phaeton (Touring)
710	Roadster	760-A	Cabriolet
720	Coupe (Club)	760-B	Cabriolet (Club)
730-A	Fordor Sedan (Standard)	770-A	Coupe (Standard) (5 Window)
730-B	Fordor Sedan (De Luxe)	770-B	Coupe (De Luxe) (5 Window)

Also, Station Wagon (listed commercially) Type 790

The 85 HP V-8 block finally underwent a change that had been suggested years earlier. Water pumps were relocated to inlet side of system at the front of the block, then forcing cooler water instead of sucking hot water through the block.
21 stud heads, without water-pump mounts differ from earlier heads. For a time, at the early part of the year, blanking plates for the block-mounted pumps were available and pumps continued to be furnished mounted on the heads.

The 1937 battery was made more accessible for service by relocating it to a well formed in the firewall.

New, this year, was a compact version of the V-8. To be known as "the thrifty sixty," new lightweight, rated at 60 HP provided an economy option of up to 25 miles per gallon (Standard models only). In point of popularity, the sixty never really caught on as it was really underpowered for the weight and size of the car. The option was discontinued in 1940.

Dashboard of the '37 was updated to include a "cluster" of gauges on the left with the speedometer matching in size to the right. Starter button was installed on the left side of the dash with a solenoid under the hood. Later, Ford offered a conversion kit consisting of push-button, solenoid, and wiring for pre-1937 cars. Parking brake was moved from center to under left side of dashboard, adding legroom in center. Ignition switch was reversed from earlier style so that ON was in the "up" position. Radio head was relocated to allow for pull-out ashtray below it.

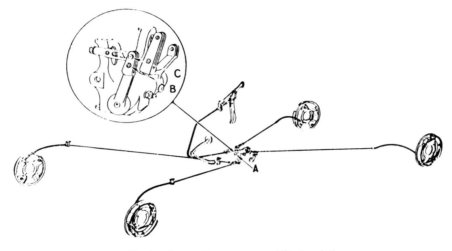

The brake system was modified, while still mechanical, a system of cables and conduits was attempted. The purpose was to reduce friction and add leverage in applying brakes. This same system lasted through 1938.

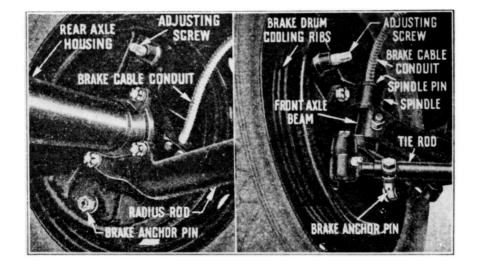

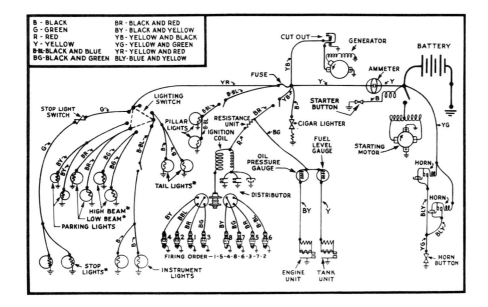

Simplified Wiring Diagram
of 1937 Ford

1937 accessory "banjo" steering wheel. Slightly different from the popular '35-'36 style at the back of the hub, this was the last year for the straight pattern of the spokes. Horn button no longer bears the V-8 of '36 and contours of light switch have become rounded. Compare with picture bottom page 146.

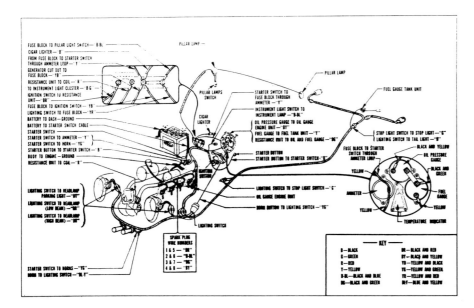

1937 Phantom Electrical System

1937 Type 770-B DeLuxe five-window Coupe

1937 Type 700-D DeLuxe Tudor Sedan

Cleaner straighter lines
of the '37 front end.

1937 Type 750 Phaeton: Mr. Max Wilkins, Hornell, New York

The windshield of the
Phaeton did not open.

Lines of canvas top were distinctly
different from earlier Phaetons and
resembled the 1936 convertible sedan.

Dashboard had no knob
for opening the windshield. Small
knob at top center operated
the wiper motor. Clock was
an accessory.

Tonneau cover was an accessory.
Note lines of forward edge of
the canvas top and compare with
that of 1936 (page 144).

Spare tire is now
mounted within the
integral trunk. With
the exception of a
few special models,
the spare was enclosed
on all body styles.

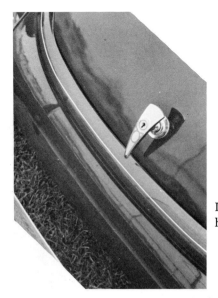

Distinctive locking
handle for integral trunk.

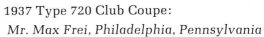

1937 Type 720 Club Coupe:
Mr. Max Frei, Philadelphia, Pennsylvania

A rare body style, this six passenger model was introduced this year.

1937 Type 730-D Fordor DeLuxe Touring Sedan (85 HP)

1937 Type 730-A Fordor Standard Sedan (60 HP)

1937 Type 730-C Fordor Standard Touring Sedan (60 HP)

The 1937 Standard 60 HP resembled the DeLuxe but lacked the chromed grill. The rear view mirror was an accessory.

For the last time, the rear tail-lamps were distinct, individual, lamp assemblies bolted on the rear fenders.

"Slantback" body had distinctly compact apearance when contrasted with touring (trunk) style.

A feature of the '37 was the redesign of the headlamps, now incorporated into the fender. Also, new was the somewhat less ornate bumper and guard.

Black-painted Standard grill (shown here) was chromed on DeLuxe models.

Internal construction of fender-mounted headlamps allowed for beam adjustment from the front of the car.

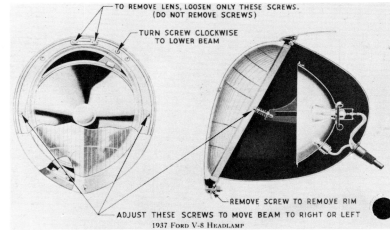

TO REMOVE LENS, LOOSEN ONLY THESE SCREWS. (DO NOT REMOVE SCREWS)

TURN SCREW CLOCKWISE TO LOWER BEAM

REMOVE SCREW TO REMOVE RIM

ADJUST THESE SCREWS TO MOVE BEAM TO RIGHT OR LEFT

1937 Ford V-8 Headlamp

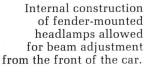

The fender reverted to a one-piece, more "streamlined" design. Horns were concealed behind, the center grill and the horn grill of '36 was eliminated.

Tudor Sedan followed lines of the "slant-backed" 1936, but, for the first time, included an externally approached luggage space. Hinged from the top, a handle at the lower part of lid released the latch and the lid could be swung up (as shown). A mechanical latch held the lid open. The gasoline cap seems more obvious, due to relocation and redesign of tail-lamp. Storage space was not as spacious as that of Touring Sedan trunk (shown below), and the spare wheel occupied must of the room.

Interior of trunk of Touring Sedan. With the "hump" back, additional space was created in the storage compartment. Spare wheel could lay flat with wooden shelf snaped over it to provide fair storage room. The tools were contained below floorboards.

179

1937

Featured this year was a split windshield, employed for the first time by Ford. Unusual was the fact that it could be opened, similarly to the earlier one-piece windshield. Hinges at the top enabled a cranking mechanism, operated by a knob on the dashboard, to force bottom of frame out. Grill ornament was adorned with engine type (either 60 or 85 hp).

Also new this year were the straight bumpers, the integral headlamps, and the split rear window. The most important new feature was the all-steel body with the final elimination of the fabric insert top.

Cleaned-up front end had a
massive appearance. Fog lamps
were an accessory. This car is an
85 hp DeLuxe model.

Retained was the cowl
ventilator. The
running board trim
was included only on
DeLuxe models.

Available with either trunk or
rumble, the five window coupe
was a popular body style.

Hub caps were similar to 1936, but reversed the earlier style. Lettering was now raised, and the area surrounding letters was painted body color. Tires are 6:00 x 16, beauty rings are optional accessories.

Running boards were flared at forward edge. Note contrast with '36 style.

The split windshield could be opened to provide ventilation.

Door handles were curved and more ornate than the straight handles of early '36 and 1935.

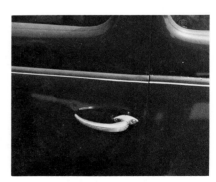

A single windshield wiper motor cleared driver's side only. The hole above windshield was for a radio antenna, missing on this car. 1937 was the first year for the antenna in this location.

Hood ornament
served as latch handle
for the hood. Turning
the ornament releases
latch.

Bumper guard is
slender with horns
behind the center
grill, no horn grills
were supplied.

Hood was hinged at the rear
and raises from the front, a distinct
difference from the "one side
or the other" of earlier years.

This was the last year for
"separate" tail-lamps bolted to
the fenders.

Painted grill inserts
replace trim louvres
of earlier years.

Some accessories apparent on this accessory-loaded 1937 Fordor are shown. They included fog lamps, bumper guards, right hand windshield wiper, spot light, mirror, bumper guards, grill guard, and headlamp treatment (see next page).

Illuminated hood ornament was a rare accessory.

Fender marker risers were accessories.

Unusual spotlight/rear view
mirror combination is shown in
this view of rare accessory,
possibly of a later vintage.

Sealed beam conversion kit,
emphasized by "lid" over the
beams, add to the list of
accessories along with fog lamps.

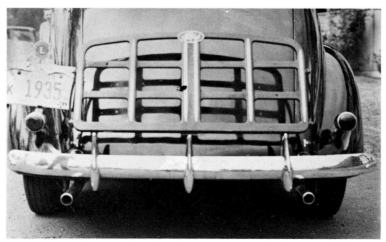

External 1937 style luggage rack increased storage space beyond
capacity of built-in trunk. Back window in 1937 was
two-piece. This was last year for license plate bracket mounted
on tail light.

1938

For the first time, in 1938, "DeLuxe" appears to have become a "line" of the Ford car rather than merely a trim option. In addition to the very wide differences in front end treatment, some body styles were available only in the DeLuxe line. Also, for the first time, the Station Wagon is now included in the list of passenger cars available.

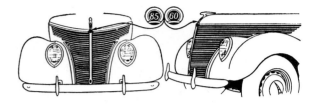

MODEL 81A FORD DELUXE *85 HP. 8-Cylinder Engine (112" Wheelbase)			**MODEL 81A FORD STANDARD** *85 HP. 8-Cylinder Engine **MODEL 82A FORD 60 HP. 8-Cylinder Engine** (112" Wheelbase)	

BODY TYPE	NAME		BODY TYPE	NAME
700-B	De Luxe Tudor Sedan		760-B	De Luxe Convertible Club Coupe
700-C	Standard Tudor Sedan		770-A	Standard (5-Window) Coupe
720	De Luxe Club Coupe		770-B	De Luxe (5-Window) Coupe
730-B	De Luxe Fordor Sedan		770-C	Standard (5-Window) Coupe (with pickup)
730-C	Standard Fordor Sedan		780-A	Standard Sedan Delivery
740	De Luxe Convertible Sedan		780-B	De Luxe Sedan Delivery
750	De Luxe Phaeton		790	Station Wagon
760-A	De Luxe Convertible Coupe			
*Listed throughout Catalogue as 90 HP.				

Commencing in 1938 the Standard model of each
year greatly resembled the DeLuxe model of the
preceding year. DeLuxe grill (right) is new, but the
grill of the Standard, shown in advertisement
below, is essentially a face lifting job
on the deluxe 1937.

*"Jonesboro? . . . Well, it's 25,
maybe 26 miles—'bout one
gallon o' gas in your Ford '60'"*

A NEW STANDARD of operating economy has been created by the new Ford V-8 with thrifty 60-horsepower engine.
Letters pour in from owners reporting 22 to 27 miles a gallon—or even more. Price tags are low too. Save money the
day you buy and every mile you drive. Enjoy the smoothness and satisfaction only *eight* cylinders can give. **FORD V·8**

1938

Cutaway view of the 85 hp transmission contrasts with that of the 60 hp gear box. Sixty bellhousing was somewhat smaller and required smaller gearbox, but design, naturally followed that of the larger engine.

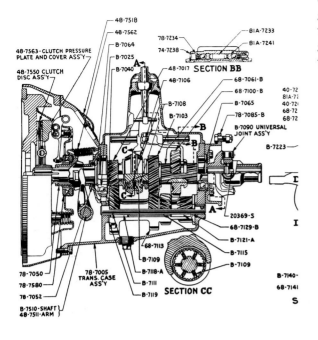

Several changes were made along the way in internal parts. Starting in 1935, the "48-" parts shown here were incorporated. With a wider main drive gear, it became necessary that the synchronizer sleeve be more narrow. Then, starting in 1936, helical-cut low and reverse gears were adopted. 1938 saw still another change in the main drive gear and synchronizer sleeve.

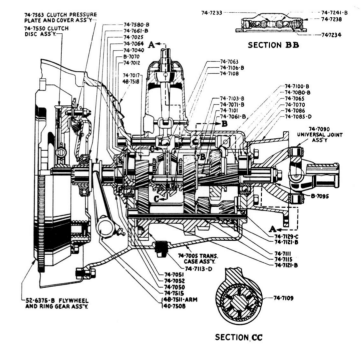

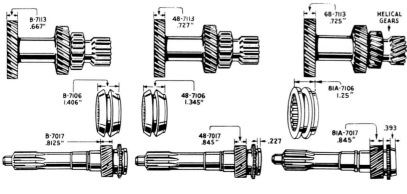

TRANSMISSION CHANGES

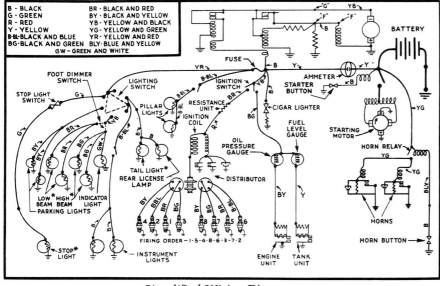

1938's battery was contained, like 1937, in shelf inset into firewall.

Simplified Wiring Diagram
of the 1938 Ford

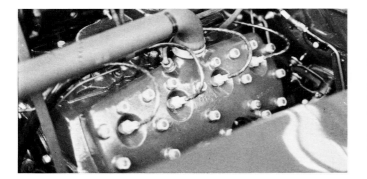

With the introduction, in 1938, of the "24 stud" engine, the cylinder head bolt pattern is seen to vary from the earlier "21 stud" engines. All 60 hp engines had 17 stud heads. Note new location for the water temperature probe just ahead of water outlet. The 1937 head, (still 21 stud but without water pump mountings), also accommodated probe in this location.

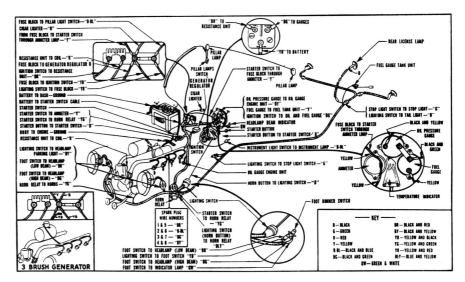

Phantom electrical system
1938 V-8

In addition to a great difference in front end treatment there was also a wide difference in the body lines between Standard and DeLuxe Tudor and Fordor sedans. Also new this year was a header-mounted radio antenna which could be rotated into a secured position by a knob inside. The windshield wipers were driven by separate right- and left-handed motors.

1938 Type 730-B DeLuxe Fordor Sedan: *Mr. Don Criteser, Oregon City, Oregon*

Rear body lines of DeLuxe
Fordor Sedan displays a smooth
outward curving slope.

Standard Fordor Sedan had a
"hump-backed" trunk
of last year's "touring Sedan".

A T-headed handle of some
elaborate design secured the trunk
lid and contained a keylock
to guard against theft.
License plate bracket is now
moved from the fender to a
position above handle. A light
was built into the handle.

1938

Rear quarter window on DeLuxe models pivot open for increased ventilation.

Standard model's rear quarter window did not open.

1938 Type 730-B Standard Fordor Sedan: *Mr. Donald Trunick, Palos Verdes Peninsula, California*

Relatively sharp "prow" of the
'38 Standard greatly resembles
that of the '37 model.

Stylized hood ornament of '38
Standard incorporates familiar Ford script
with V-8. "60" indicates use of the
sixty horsepower engine, otherwise
"85" would appear.

'38 Standard grill greatly
resembles that of the '37
DeLuxe, but is painted
black. Three horizontal
bands of dress-up chrome
were furnished on the
85 hp models.

Rear view of '38 Standard Fordor
shows use of
two tail lamps, '38 style.

1938

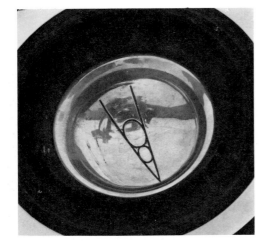

Hub caps displayed highly stylized V-8.
Wheels were unchanged and
tires remained at 6:00 x 16.

1938 Type 740 DeLuxe Convertible Sedan

Although very similar to '37's front end,
lines have been blunted somewhat
by trim changes. Missing is one of the
bumper guards which became standard
issue this year, not accessories.

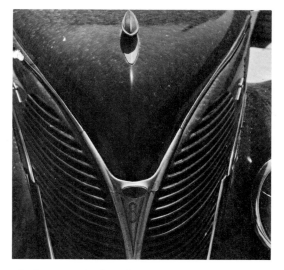

As in 1937, the hood ornament serves as a latching handle for the hood. Turning handle (see below) released the latch and hood could be raised. All DeLuxe models were available only with the 85 hp "big" engine (listed throughout catalogs as 90 hp), but the Standards were available with either the 85 or the "thrifty sixty".

Pilot light (above starter button) on left of dashboard advised when "high" beam of headlamp was on. Also new this year was a floor-mounted, foot-operated, dimmer switch. Design of spokes in banjo wheel is quite different from earlier '35-'37 styles.

Convertible Sedan windshield does not open. Radio speaker has been moved to dashboard where it is now flanked by controls.

Built-in defroster vents served with forced air from heater fan eliminated need for accessory steering post mounted fans or accessory heater ducts.

1938 headlamp is only changed a little
from 1937 style (insert),
but the two are not interchangeable.

Taillamp, as the separate item for 1937
(insert), has disappeared entirely
and is now merely a trim assembly
located directly on the rear fenders.

Leather pad cushions top
assembly when lowered; top
saddles have once again
disappeared.

Interior trim and dashboard are
wood-grained. Seats are genuine leather
and door panels are trimmed with
artificial leather.

Windows, when rolled up, and
compartment sealed off with removable
pillars (as seen on page 136) provide
all of the comfort of a closed car.

1939

MODEL 91A FORD DELUXE
*85 HP. 8-Cylinder Engine
(112″ Wheelbase)

BODY TYPE	NAME	BODY TYPE	NAME
70-A	Standard Tudor Sedan	76	De Luxe Convertible Coupe
70-B	De Luxe Tudor Sedan	77-A	Standard (5-Window) Coupe
73-A	Standard Fordor Sedan	77-B	De Luxe (5-Window) Coupe
73-B	De Luxe Fordor Sedan	78	Sedan Delivery
74	De Luxe Convertible Fordor Sedan	79	Station Wagon

*Listed throughout Catalogue as 90 HP.

MODEL 91A FORD STANDARD *85 HP. 8-Cylinder Engine

MODEL 922A FORD 60 HP. 8-Cylinder Engine
(112″ Wheelbase)

Note different bumper guards between DeLuxe and Standard. Bumpers were otherwise the same.

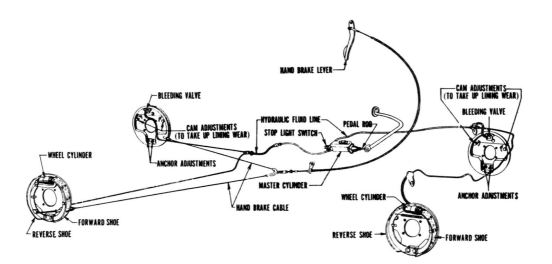

After resisting the change for years, Ford's biggest surprise of 1939 was the addition of "hydraulic brakes". Basically, the difference is that all of the mechanical linkage and rods between the pedal and the wheel have been replaced with oil, steel tubes, a master cylinder, and an activating cylinder at each wheel. Pressure on the master cylinder, applied by pressing the pedal, caused the wheel cylinders to activate the shoes against the drums. Far less pedal pressure was thus required with these brakes and the basic system has remained unchanged since.

1939 Ford carburetor. Throttle-cam pertrudes below mounting flange and carburetor will not therefore stand alone on a flat surface.

'39 DeLuxe saw a relocation of the fan from the front of the generator, to the forward, lengthened, extension of the crankshaft. Standard models retained fan on generator for this year.

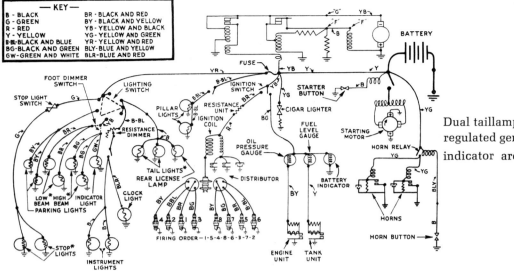

Dual taillamps and two-brush regulated generator with battery indicator are included.

Simplified wiring diagram 1939 DeLuxe Ford V-8.

DeLuxe line has a new frontal treatment.

Ford V-8 with single taillamp, three brush generator, cut-out and conventional ammeter, typical of the '39 Standard models.

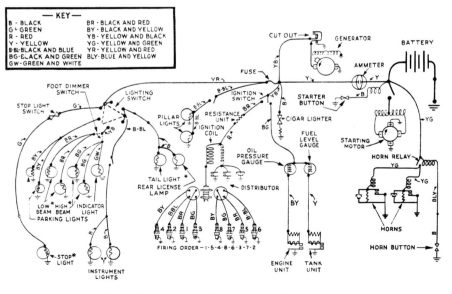

Simplified wiring diagram 1939 Standard

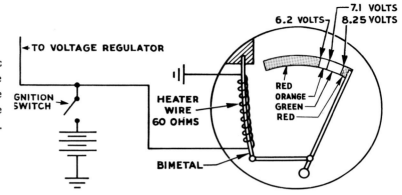

Battery indicator was bi-metallic operated instrument displaying intelligence based on sensing the operation of the voltage regulator. Used only in the DeLuxe Line.

Standard front end resembles the 1938 DeLuxe series.

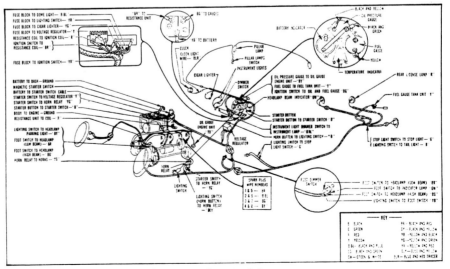

Phantom Electrical System
1939 DeLuxe Ford V-8

1939 Type 73-B DeLuxe Fordor Sedan: *Mr. Richard Falk, Walnut Creek, California*

A single, unidirectional, wiper motor mounted between the two panes and operating through a series of eccentric linkages, operated both wiper blades.

Spider wheelcovers and outside
rear view mirrors are accessories.

Spare tire, placed in luggage compartment, still leaves ample storage space.
Rear bumpers were alike in 1938 and 1939,
but guards, now standard, differed on
'39 DeLuxe from '38 and '39 Standard.

Rare windwing accessory from
Ford (outside mirror is also
accessory). Note unusual shape
of the rear edge of glass.

This is a three passenger car.

1939 Type 77-B DeLuxe five window coupe: *Mr. Al Rogers, Portland, Oregon*

Large trunk offers substantial storage space and made this model a popular businessman's car.

Massive appearance of the '39 front end is distinctive.

Clean lines of '39 dashboard show last of the crank-out windshield knobs and floor-mounted gearshift. Grill for radio is unoccupied; controls would replace plate below grill. Moved from steering wheel, "high" (country) driving beam is controlled by switch on floor, indicator beam is furnished over the starter button.

Although '39 Standard did use the same lens as the '38 (right), '39 DeLuxe differs.

Sloping lines of rear deck are distinctive. This is the last year for this wheel with the 10 ¼″ bolt centers. Tires are 6:00 x 16.

1939 Type 79 Standard Station Wagon: *Mr. Donald Lopez, Concord, California*

Frontal treatment greatly resembles the 1938 DeLuxe model, although it is trimmed differently.

Beauty of design is enduring. Wooden body follows classic lines. Note similarity to earlier (1936) body style, below.

1939

This was the last model
with the exposed rumble seat.

1939 Type 76 DeLuxe Convertible Coupe: *Mr. Donald Criteser, Oregon City, Oregon*

Note whip antenna over windshield. Rear view mirror is accessory.

Accessory spider hubcaps add to trim of car. Rumble is upholstered in leatherette and has rubber mat. Interior is genuine leather.

Accessory Oil Bath Air Cleaner installed on carburetor. More often seen on trucks, this type was employed on passenger cars as well in excessively dusty usage. Contrast with more common style (lower right).

Battery on DeLuxe models has been relocated to fender well from firewall. However, in standard models of 1939, battery remained on the firewall.

1939 Type 74 DeLuxe Convertible Sedan: *Mr. Al Rogers, Portland, Oregon*

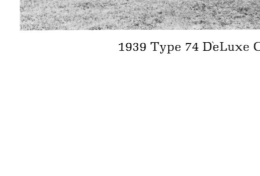

This is the last year in which
the Convertible four-door Sedan
was made.

Removable center pillars
(between windows) offer extra
good looks of an open car.
Genuine leather seats are set off
by canvas top.

Ten snap fasteners on each
side secure top, four secure
lower rear, six more are spaced
along rails above windows.

Rear window flap has been
dropped in these photos. Glass
size is approximately 6 x 20" and
is contained in chromed frame.

Latching trunk handle has
become less ornate than the '38
style (insert). Taillamps are
identical to '38.

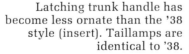

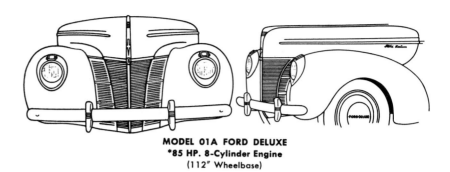

MODEL 01A FORD DELUXE
*85 HP. 8-Cylinder Engine
(112" Wheelbase)

BODY TYPE	NAME	BODY TYPE	NAME
66	De Luxe Convertible Club Coupe	73-B	De Luxe Fordor Sedan
67-A	Standard Business Coupe	77-A	Standard (5-Window) Coupe
67-B	De Luxe Business Coupe	77-B	De Luxe (5-Window) Coupe
70-A	Standard Tudor Sedan	78	De Luxe Sedan Delivery
70-B	De Luxe Tudor Sedan	79-A	Standard Station Wagon
73-A	Standard Fordor Sedan	79-B	De Luxe Station Wagon

*Listed throughout Catalogue as 90 HP.

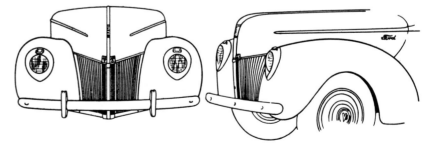

MODEL 01A FORD—STANDARD *85 HP. 8-Cylinder Engine
MODEL 022A FORD—60 HP. 8-Cylinder Engine
(112" Wheelbase)

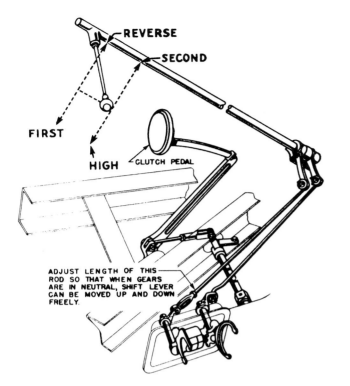

REVERSE

SECOND

FIRST

HIGH

CLUTCH PEDAL

ADJUST LENGTH OF THIS ROD SO THAT WHEN GEARS ARE IN NEUTRAL, SHIFT LEVER CAN BE MOVED UP AND DOWN FREELY.

New this year was a gearshift lever mounted on the Steering Column and which deleted the lever at the center of the front seat. An entirely new linkage was thus required below the floorboards to achieve this shift. So new was the approach, that it was then necessary for Ford to furnish shifting instructions with each car.

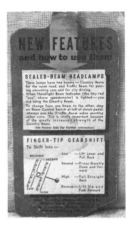

Also new in 1940 was the introduction of sealed beam headlamps, although their location in the fenders was unchanged. Greatly increasing the lamp brilliance, these sealed bulbs were adjustable for beam deflection within their holders, as shown below. Sealed beams increase candle power from 27 to almost 40 cp.

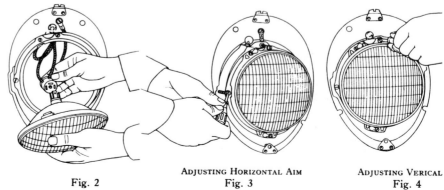

Fig. 2

ADJUSTING HORIZONTAL AIM
Fig. 3

ADJUSTING VERICAL
Fig. 4

1940 Type 66 DeLuxe Convertible Coupe: *Mr. Ed Weidner, Sacramento, California*

DeLuxe front end;
grill guard is an accessory.

Headlamps are fitted with smart new chrome rims. Long line of hood emphasises smartness of design.

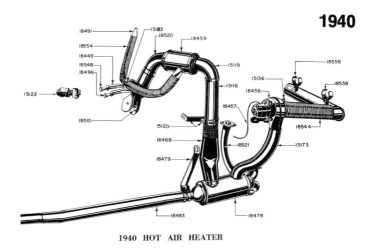

1940 HOT AIR HEATER

1940 saw the introduction of the first automatically-operated top on Ford Convertibles. Two 4½″ inch vacuum cylinders operated by manifold vacuum were employed to lower and raise the top.

Radio antenna is mounted over windshield which, for the first time, cannot be opened.

Rear window is approximately 6 x 20″ and rear flap can be lowered.

An interested accessory is the hot air manifold heater shown here. Exhaust gases are deflected through a heat exchanger around which is ducted the incoming air to be heated and forced through tubes and deflectors to the passenger compartment.

1940

Parking lamp is 1.5 cp bulb in receptacle placed behind ingeniously designed lens above headlamp.

Accessory grill guard protects grill and looks well. Hood latch is released by lifting handle at front center of hood.

New this year is the addition of wind vents. Manually operated, they were furnished with latching mechanism shown. On closed cars, divider strip lowered with window.

Steel 16″ wheels with the five mounting lugs spaced on a 5½″ circle were new this year eliminating the need for the wider hub cap. 1940 hubcap is the chromed section only, there is no "skirt" on the cap. Tires are 6:00 x 16.

Door handle has become quite "streamlined". Keylock on curbside door only.

Front seats tilt forward to allow easy access to wide rear passenger bench seat.

The unique 1940 rear lamp assembly used both on DeLuxe (2) and Standard (1) cars.

Tail lamps are standard on both rear fenders in the DeLuxe Series.

Door handles and window risers
are plastic-dipped, not chromed.

Two-spoke steering wheel is new for '40.
Antenna "lead" is a chromed rod
supported between insulated standoffs
between the windshield panes.

Rear window section is secured by row
of fasteners across the top and
held securely in place by two
leather straps (one of which is visible).
Flap can be lowered by undoing
straps and fasteners.

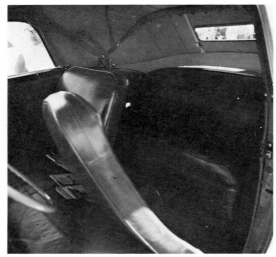

Leather seat is sewn with
great care; corners and seams
are butted.

Eliminated is the knob at
center of dashboard as well as
mechanism for cranking
windshield open. Radio is now
an integral package
behind the grill.

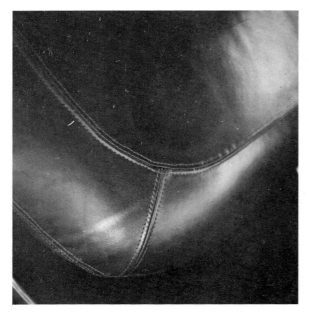

Top assembly is secured by three chromed latching mechanisms.

Differences in ashtray indicate earlier style (far right) in which lid raised to expose tray, and later (near right) in which entire tray tilts out for use. Locking release button for glove compartment door has been moved off the lid for the first time this year.

1940 trunk lid handle differs from earlier styles.

1940 Bumper guards were same for DeLuxe and Standard series.

1940

1940 Type 79-B DeLuxe Station Wagon: *Mrs. Charles Leffingwell, Cardiff-by-the-Sea, California*

Spotlight and rear view mirror are accessories. Dual windshield wipers are operated from one unidirectional motor through series of mechanical links.

Rear fenders are same in station wagons from 1938-1940.

Rear bumper guards have been added. Station wagon omitted rear guards due to interference with tailgate when lowered. Unique to DeLuxe model this year is a two-piece back window. Standard model had one large pane.

1940

Hood latch is released by pulling handle in hood center trim.

This is last year for traditional cowl ventilators.

Spotlight is a desirable accessory model. Trim escutcheon merely reads "Ford" on Standard models.

Glassed all around, the rear
doors have sliding panes.

A dome light, operated by a
switch at the lamp, is provided.

Front doors, paneled in wood, have metal
plate holding latch and window risers.

Rear door locks seem not to have
changed greatly from style reported in
1936. (See page 143).

Control handle for rotating and
tilting the accessory spotlight extends
through cowl post.

DeLuxe series instrument
cluster is plastic-trimmed.

Clean lines of '40 DeLuxe instrument
panel are accentuated by column-
mounted gear shift and open space where
gear shift lever previously was placed.

Starter button remains on dash,
located to right of ashtray.

Headlamp (and parking) control switch
has been moved to dashboard from
steering wheel where it joins choke,
throttle, and cigar lighter. Radio, when
used, had controls located in place of trim
plate above dash.

Clock, an accessory item, is fitted
into glove box door. Keylock button
above is compartment lid latch control.

Rear window swings out and is held by thumb wheel tightened on track.

Roof of station wagon is treated canvas stretched over wooden slats, clearly seen in this view.

Bottom edge of rear window has rubber flap to protect against weather.

1940

Hub of two spoke
Standard steering wheel
lacks plastic trim of the
DeLuxe series.

Dashboard of the 1940 Standard differs
from that of the DeLuxe model, which
employed more plastic (then a fairly new
product) trim. Instrument cluster,
while compact and practical, had less
modernity than did the DeLuxe style
shown below.

Radio grill of center section
appears to be about the same as
the DeLuxe model, although the
trim of that series is more fancy.

Dashboard of the 1940 DeLuxe series.

Glove compartment lid is quite
austere compared to DeLuxe series
shown on page 219.

1940 Type 70-A Standard Tudor Sedan:
Mr. Gary Walcher, La Mesa, California

1940 Type 73-B DeLuxe Fordor Sedan:
Mr. Carl Burnett, San Diego, California

Standard (left) lacks taillamp
on right fender.

DeLuxe grill (upper)
differs from that of
Standard, and in this view,
the additional difference
in shape of the hoods is
apparent. '40 Standard
greatly resembles the
'39 DeLuxe.

Standard escutcheon plate differs, not only in text, but in size as seen clearly in this comparative view.

Standard headlamp, while incorporating sealed beams, remains less impressive, and is painted rather than chromed as is DeLuxe (lower).

In this very original Fordor, an original, Ford script tire remains in the trunk, recessed into the floor. Also, original is the rubber trunk floor mat.

In rear view, Standard and DeLuxe are very similar (but for right hand tail lamp).

1940 Type 73-B DeLuxe Fordor Sedan: *Mr. John Speegle, Stockton, California*
Rear quarter windows pivot open on DeLuxe, are stationary on Standard models.

1940 Type 77-B DeLuxe 5 Window Coupe

Rear view of the 5-window coupe is very similar to that of same type in 1939 but redesigned tail lamps are a major difference. See page 204.

Rear quarter window does not open.

Sealed beam headlamps, first employed in 1940 model, provided almost twice as much light. A floor-mounted beam switch was provided, and for the first time a circuit breaker was furnished in place of the fuse.

Distinctive tail lamp trim and redesigned trunk handle differ from previous year.

Closed cars were trimmed in long-wearing bedford cord. DeLuxe model handles and window risers were plastic-dipped. Outside surface of door had smooth curved lines.

A feature of the 5 window coupe was the installation of two rather small seats for additional passengers behind the front seat. 5-window Business Coupe featured a large package shelf in place of seats.

"Ventilators" in forward section of front door glass opened out manually and were fitted with dog-legged eccentric latches.

Battery is now contained in shelf
located under hood, as was
'39 DeLuxe.

Voltage Regulator, introduced on
1939 DeLuxe models, is now
standard and is located on firewall.

1940 Chassis — Note linkage of column shift.

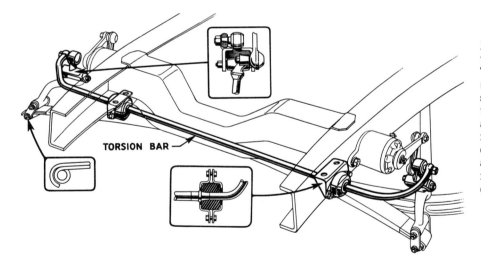

Early models of the 1940 Ford were equipped with a new Torsion type ride stabilizer (below). However, this was shortly abandoned in favor of the later type (left) which was anchored by flanges (see insert at right) to prevent side movement of the frame with respect to the axle. These stabilizers improved riding comfort and steering control.

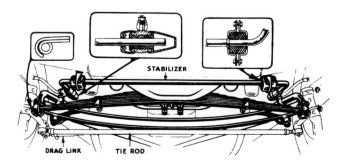

1941

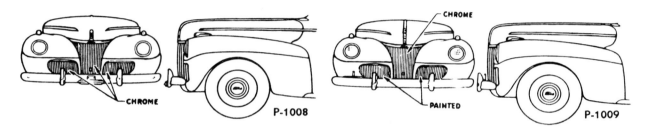

MODEL 11A FORD SUPER DELUXE
90 HP. 8-Cylinder Engine

MODEL 11A FORD DELUXE
90 HP. 8-Cylinder Engine

BODY TYPE	NAME	BODY TYPE	NAME
67-A	De Luxe Coupe (with auxiliary seats)	73-B	Super De Luxe Fordor Sedan
67-B	Super De Luxe Coupe (with auxiliary seats)	73-C	Special Fordor Sedan
70-A	De Luxe Tudor Sedan	76	Super De Luxe Convertible Club Coupe
70-B	Super De Luxe Tudor Sedan	77-A	De Luxe (5-Window) Coupe
70-C	Special Tudor Sedan	77-B	Super De Luxe (5-Window) Coupe
72	Super De Luxe Sedan Coupe	77-C	Special Coupe (5-Window)
73-A	De Luxe Fordor Sedan	79-A	De Luxe Station Wagon
		79-B	Super De Luxe Station Wagon

1941 saw a major styling and body redesign, and a two-inch increase in wheelbase to 114". New for this year is the Special line which is limited to a six-cylinder in-line engine which replaced the 60 hp V-8. Body style is essentially that of the DeLuxe and Super DeLuxe lines but for trim, but Special line is not properly to be included in this work on the V-8 engines. The Six cylinder engine was available in the Special line exclusively, and the DeLuxe line optionally.

234

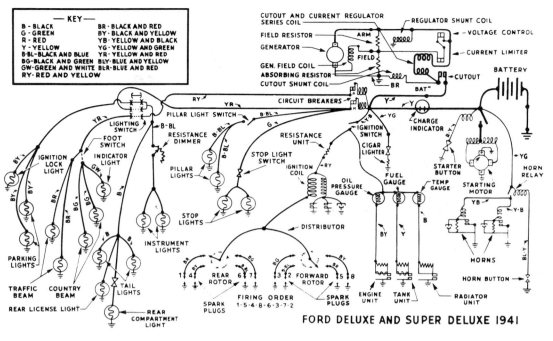

Wiring diagram of 1941 Ford DeLuxe and Super DeLuxe

Super DeLuxe became a new top-of-the-line series. Next, the DeLuxe, and additionally the Special which was a somewhat stripped-down car for the economy buyer with a six cylinder in-line engine.

1941 fender was no longer one piece. Trim strip hides parting line on the Super DeLuxe models. This construction, with the horizontal parting line was only used for this one year.

1941 Type 67-A DeLuxe 5 Window Coupe (5 passenger): *Mr. Jack Foster, Portland, Oregon*

Super DeLuxe front end (facing page) had
additional trim strips concealing the fender parting
lines as well as its designation in an escutcheon
on the left fender. DeLuxe models (right)
had painted outer grills, rather than chromed, and
no trim on the fender seam.

1941 DeLuxe Front View

1941 Type 77-B Super DeLuxe 5 Window Coupe (3 passenger):

Mr. David Ruesch, Los Angeles, California

1941 Super DeLuxe Front View

Rear bumper center guard (which hides Ford script) is an accessory but dual exhaust pipes are not correct for the car. The year's substantial redesign of the body style extends to the taillamps too.

Wider bodies were further accentuated by sweep of lower door which overhangs much of the running board. Compare lower door lines with 1940 door on page 231.

The door, when closed, now sweeps over the running board, almost concealing it.

A roof-mounted antenna serves the radio, and the wind deflectors are now a crank-out style. The outside rear view mirror is an accessory.

Rear window has become a one-piece type again and on closed cars is slightly convex. Neither it nor the rear quarter windows can be opened.

The roof-mounted, telescoping antenna
is fixed, can be collapsed, but not rotated.

New this year is a cable-connected
hood release knob under the dashboard.
Gone was the mechanical release at the
front of the hood.

"Separate" parking lamps
made their return this year.

Rear fenders have been "budged" out and gasoline filler neck and cap is now located within access door in left rear fender. Some, not all, DeLuxe models were furnished without right-hand taillamp.

Taillamps have again been restyled and have the appearance of being "separate" although this is not the case.

1941

Bumper-mounted grill guard is accessory, as are interesting bumper end trim plates. Two chrome grills on either side of center grill are painted black for DeLuxe series.

1941 Type 76 Super DeLuxe Convertible Club Coupe:

Mrs. Rita Schmeiser, Columbia River, Washington

"Super DeLuxe' 'insignia is omitted on DeLuxe line.

1941 saw a significant change in styling. Contrast rounded, fuller, body style with the somewhat smaller and more compact style of 1940 (insert). A two inch increase in length between front and rear wheels added length. Design changes added width and interior room. Detail improvements included a keylock for the door on the driver's side. Missing is the chrome trim at fender parting line, correct for Super DeLuxe line.

In addition to accessory beauty rings, these wheels show striping trim of wheels not ordinarily found.

Wider body caused door to overhang the running boards.

Smooth lines of rear deck conceal a generous storage compartment.

Two-spoke steering wheel is now fittted with unique semi-circular horn ring. A knob, to right and below starter button, is hood release.

Design of rear deck lid handle has undergone still another revision.

MODEL 21A FORD SUPER DELUXE
90 HP. 8-Cylinder Engine
(114" Wheelbase)

MODEL 21A FORD DELUXE
90 HP. 8-Cylinder Engine

BODY TYPE	NAME	BODY TYPE	NAME
70-A	De Luxe Tudor Sedan	73-C	Special Fordor Sedan
70-B	Super De Luxe Tudor Sedan	76	Super De Luxe Convertible Club Coupe
70-C	Special Tudor Sedan	77-A	De Luxe (5-Window) Coupe
72-A	De Luxe Sedan Coupe	77-B	Super De Luxe (5-Window) Coupe
72-B	Super De Luxe Sedan Coupe	77-C	Special Coupe (5-Window)
73-A	De Luxe Fordor Sedan	78	De Luxe Sedan Delivery
73-B	Super De Luxe Fordor Sedan	79-B	Super De Luxe Station Wagon

Again in 1942 there was a Special line limited to the six cylinder
engine and otherwise quite similar in appearance to the DeLuxe and the Super
DeLuxe lines. Not properly to be included in this work on the V-8 engines, the
six cylinder engine was available in the Special line exclusively and the
DeLuxe line optionally.

How Defense Needs have been met and Ford Quality improved

As DEFENSE PRODUCTION has gained pace, many people have wondered about its effect on 1942 cars. Would shortages of some materials force substitutes into the motor car? Would buyers get less quality for their money this year? For our part at Ford, we are glad to say that defense requirements have been met in full without a single reduction in the goodness of the car mechanically—and with many real improvements in its beauty, comfort and performance. Some new materials have replaced old ones, generally at greater cost to us. In every case, the new is equal to or better than the old. Here are instances of what we have done . . .

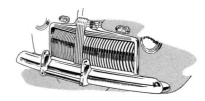

Steel Stampings for Die-Castings

Exterior parts like radiator grilles, and mechanical parts like generators and starter end plates, are now made from steel stampings instead of die-castings, without affecting their usefulness or appearance. This has freed large amounts of zinc, aluminum and other defense-needed materials.

Plastics Replace Metal for Interior Trim

We have been developing plastics for a long time at Ford. The value of this is now apparent. The wider use of plastics this year in instrument panel, radio grille, door handles and other interior trim has released large quantities of zinc formerly used in metal die-castings, as well as nickel and chromium formerly used in plating bright metal parts. The plastic parts are lighter in weight, fully as serviceable, and very attractive in appearance.

Molybdenum Replaces Nickel

Nickel is important not only in the finish of plated metal but in improving the toughness of steel. In defense production it is used in the manufacture of aviation engine parts and armor plate. Ford valves, transmission gears, shafts, and many other parts formerly containing nickel, are now alloyed with molybdenum and chromium. For the purpose, these parts are as good as or better than those replaced.

Some Results in Defense Metals Saved

Based on present conditions, here are some examples of how new materials and methods in the 1942 Ford are helping relieve defense "shortages." Figures show the *cut* in use this year of the materials named:

Primary (*new*) Aluminum has been cut out 100% . . . Secondary (*re-melted*) Aluminum has been cut down 70% . . . Nickel has been cut down by 90.7% . . . Magnesium, cut out almost entirely, is down 98.7% . . . Zinc has been reduced by 37.5% . . . Copper, Tin, Lead, and Tungsten cut down in varying amounts from 5.2% to 81%.

America's Most Modern 6...America's Lowest-priced 8

1942 Type 77-B Super DeLuxe (5 window) Coupe

Photos of 1942 coupe courtesy of Harrah's Automobile Collection.

Front end of car shows effects of economy metal drives. Although superficially resembling the 1941 model (insert), grill has been enlarged to present more massive effect. A stone shield has been added between bumper and body. This is a relatively early '42. Later models had less chrome, trim was painted.

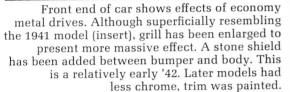

Fender is again simplified and no longer has wide horizontal trim to conceal parting flange, now gone. Compare with similar view of 1941 car (insert).

Rear view of 1942 greatly resembles that of the 1941 (insert), but for new taillamp treatment.

The dashboard of 1942 differed only slightly from that of 1941. Turn indicators first appeared in kit form, on the '42 model. Also, new as an accessory this year was the vacuum operated windshield washer, complete with auxiliary vacuum tank. 1942 Super DeLuxe Station Wagon was first to have roll-up windows in rear doors.

This Super DeLuxe Fordor sedan was the last civilian vehicle to be manufactured before World War II. Built on February 10, 1942, it showed the effect of growing metal shortages. Headlamp and parking lamp rims are painted and, as with most of the last few cars, the side trim is painted rather than chromed.

photo from Ford Archives, Dearborn, Michigan

Those English Fords!!

Ford V·8

Money cannot buy a sweeter-running,

more pleasantly-handled car, and its thrilling performance

does not involve extravagant fuel-consumption, because the

eight-cylinder engine is able to do practically everything on top

gear. See All Body-Types in the Local Ford Dealer's Showroom.

He Invites You to Try Any Ford V-8, Over a Route that You Select.

Ford V-8 Touring Saloon, Double-Entrance, as illustrated, £22 . 10s. Tax, **£250** £16 . 10s. Tax, **£235**

Alternative body-types from £230 and £215, respectively.   All prices at Works.

FORD MOTOR COMPANY LIMITED, WORKS: DAGENHAM, ESSEX. LONDON SHOWROOMS: 88 REGENT STREET, W.1

In addition to the Rouge River Plant at Dearborn, "associated" Ford Companies (independent, but controlled by Ford) operated *manufacturing plants* in East Windsor, Canada, Dagenham, England, and Cologne, Germany. Canada served all of the United Kingdom, except for Great Britain, which was served by Dagenham, and Cologne served Germany, Austria, Hungary and Czechoslovakia. In addition, there were *assembly* plants in Argentina, the Canal Zone, Cuba, Peru, Mexico, Uraguay, Brazil, Chila, China, Japan, Egypt, France, Belgium, Spain, Italy, Romania, Denmark, Ireland, Finland, Turkey, Portugal, Holland, Sweden, and Greece!

In these assembly plants, parts shipped from one of the four major manufacturing companies were assembled and often the coachwork varied considerably while still bearing a strong resemblance. This was not surprising because the *basic* chassis and running gear was roughly the same for each model year.

Shown is an advertisement which appeared in the May 9, 1936 ILLUSTRATED LONDON NEWS. Note the similarity to the American '36 Ford but also note the addition of parking lamps on the front fenders as well as the unusual bumper guards.

1932-33 Convertible sedan manufactured by Ford at Cologne shows influence of German stylists. Body, by Deutsch Coach Builders, greatly resembles that of the American design but top assembly is obviously more ponderous.

1938-40 German Ford V-8 Convertible Sedan, body by Glaser, displays style and grace, but with top lowered, longer Landau irons (lower photo) offer a more cumbersome appearance. This car also has the parking lamps mounted on the fenders.

Foreign production of Ford automobiles (and trucks), while spread over a wide geographical extent contributed, however, only about ten percent of the total volume of production in the years from 1932 to 1942, according to the Company's production figures.

1932 V-8
(below, Model B)

1933 & 1934

1935

1936

1936 Spider Hub Cap
(Accessory)

CAP

IT   OFF   ! _____

1937

1939

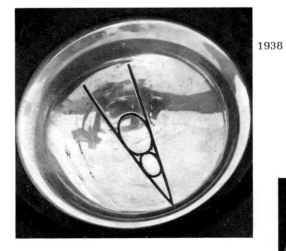

1938

1941

1940 DeLuxe (left) and Standard

255

Earliest of the 1932 fuel pumps, were similar to Model 18-9350 (shown here) which was introduced shortly after production of the V-8 began. It differed in exposed height, however, being about 1½″ shorter. Pumps mounted on horizontal flange and an oil filler tube was placed ahead of pump (below). The earlier pump had a somewhat different operating mechanism with more of the pump, thus mounted below mounting flanges.

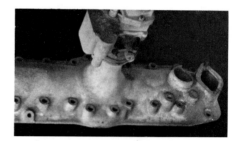

Introduced on January 1, 1934, this pump called for a modification of the manifold and eventually eliminated the separate oil filler tube altogether. Mounted on a vertical face of a die cast riser, it enabled oil filler tube to be relocated to rear of fuel pump. Same pump was then used until 1936.

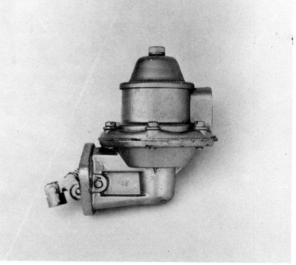

A slightly larger pump (right)
was introduced during 1936.

The fuel pump was supplied in a larger
version of the same pump during 1936.
This same pump then prevailed into 1940.
In 1941, a similar pump with a slightly
larger flange was introduced. Since the
hole pattern was unchanged is would be
possible to use that later pump on
an earlier fuel pump mounting stand,
but the earlier style if used on '41-'42
parts would cause some valve
chamber leakage.

Introduced on the '46 model, but then
specified as a universal retrofit, was a fuel
pump with a glass bowl fuel strainer
as shown here.

All pre-war passenger car generators were rated at six Volts, (12 Volt generators first appeared on Ford trucks only in 1942). The 1932 generator was mounted on a post which was secured in forward end of manifold by clamping bolt thus relatively free to rotate in mount. Generator had three brushes, one of which adjusted position for output current variation, and was equipped with a voltage sensitive cut-out to prevent reverse current to the generator from the battery.

The 1933 generator (and manifold) was changed to correct mounting problem by the design of a flanged mount secured to a stud in the manifold.

258

The 1935 generator introduced a cooling system by opening the shoulder of the case with vents and adding an integrally cast fan to the back of the pulley. Several ratings (sizes) of this model appeared depending on load requirements and it was employed through the 1939 Standard where it had grown to 28 amps from the original 12.

Introduced during 1938 and used on the '39 DeLuxe was a new system in which a Voltage Regulator was employed to vary the field current in the generator and it now became a 2-brush unit with no access cover to the interior as previously.

In 1939 on DeLuxe models, the fan was relocated to front of crankshaft and no longer was mounted at pulley (insert). By 1940, Standard models followed.

1942 mounting brought fan back to mate with generator mounting bracket as shown by extra holes in '42 generator at right.

Tall coil of 1932 is noticeably different than later styles. Reportedly a re-packaging of earlier Model A components, height of coil required especially long shaft on fan in order for blades to clear coil (below right).

Distributors on V-8 for the first time incorporated a vacuum advance of the spark which was retarded for easier starting by spring pressure. Vacuum build-up in intake manifold caused plunger to retract against spring and counterweights advanced spark. This style, used from 1933 to mid 1936 has three tapped holes for mounting the ignition coil.

Ignition coil used from 1933-36 is generally called the "dome top" coil and has three mounting holes through which screws are threaded into the distributor.

260

A rare distributor and coil, used only in late 1936. The coil is flat-topped, and has two mounting holes. Note the position of the two holes in the distributor are placed at an angle rather than straight across.

All distributors are keyed to the end of the crankshaft by means of an *offset* key on the mating flange. An attempt to secure the distributor with this key rotated a half turn out of place will almost certainly cause the housing to crack when the crank is turned.

The 1937 to 1941 style was the "two-hole" distributor in which the coil-mounting holes were located straight across the unit. Coil is taller and same assembly was used on both 85 HP and the 60 HP engine.

In 1942, distributor was finally substantially modified, and coil removed from assembly and mounted separately. Although vacuum advance is retained, balance of construction is quite different. Cap is flat disc with four wires plugged into each side.

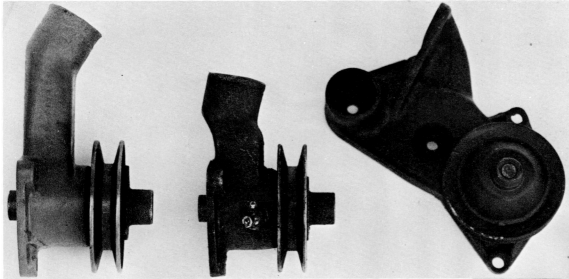

Dual water pumps were introduced on the V-8 although there were those who said from the start that they were located in the wrong place. They were incorporated at the front end of the heads and served to draw heated water from the block. Later, in 1937, the pumps were relocated to the block where they served to draw the cooler water from the radiator and thus operate in a better environment.

From the left are the "high necked" water pump used in 1932, lower style from 1933 on (without temperature gauge receptacle prior to 1935), and the type placed at the entrance to the block (in 1937). Sixty horsepower engines were similar (1937-1940) but smaller. Pump itself was common to both sides, but after 1937 mounts were right and left-handed.

1935 style water pump with tapped hole for temperature gauge probe.

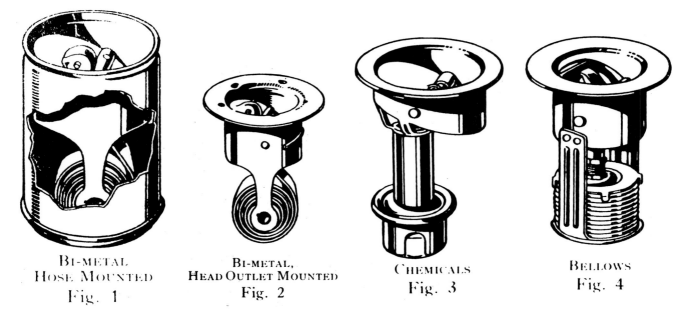

BI-METAL HOSE MOUNTED
Fig. 1

BI-METAL, HEAD OUTLET MOUNTED
Fig. 2

CHEMICALS
Fig. 3

BELLOWS
Fig. 4

In order to more quickly reach operating temperature, and to hold same, Ford introduced on the 1933 models thermostats installed in the radiator outlet hoses. These were used until early 1937 when they were redesigned and mounted in the water inlet at the block (Fig. 2). Both types were bi-metallic and were designed to start opening at 145° and be fully open at 180° F. Later in 1937, a chemical type was employed (Fig. 3) which depended on an expansion to operate a butterfly valve. Then, in 1940, a similar type, but employing an expansible fluid operating a bellows (Fig. 4). Later, in 1941, a return was made to a type of bi-metal-operated thermostat.

1932 single barrel Detroit Lubricator
carburetor mounts on flanges placed
fore-and-aft on manifold.

Dashboard throttle control rod
operates on foot accelerator linkage.

1933 carburetor (right)
has the addition of an
arm which controls
throat butterfly valve
and is connected to dash-
board thorttle knob by
linkage.

1933 carburetor is
similar to 1932 except for
hand throttle control lever.

1934 saw the introduction of a dual barrel carburetor manufactured by Stromberg and this illustration, from the 1934 sales literature, illustrates the dual manifold effect.

Dual throat marks the post 1934 carburetor (right).

1934-1935 style dual barrel downdraft carburetor.

1936-38 style is the Stromberg 97 dual barrel carburetor introduced in April of '36. This has a winter/summer adjustment of the accelerating pump throw with the linkage being adjustable at the throttle cam for either position. Winter driving conditions require the use of an additional throw of the pump arm.

The "Ford" carburetor, marked "91-99" on main body, first used on some 1938 models became standard for 1939-41 85 HP. Ford units are unusual in that throttle arm falls below mounting surface and unit cannot be placed upright on a flat surface. The 1937-38 Ford sixty used a carburetor marked "81" on main body, later, in 1939-1940 it was marked "92".

Early 1933 manifold

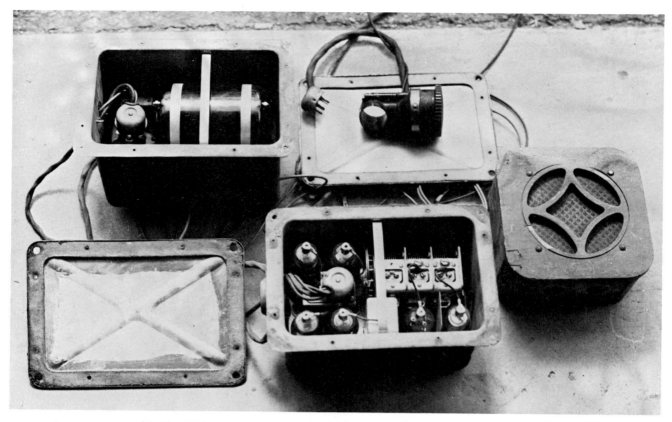

A very rare assembly, the 1932 motor-generator radio. With the control head mounted on the steering column, cables were run to the two sealed boxes which were inserted into and below the floor pan in the rear. From there, a second cable ran to the speaker mounted on the firewall. Never really popular, perhaps due to the need to deface the floorpans, these radios are extremely scarce at this time.

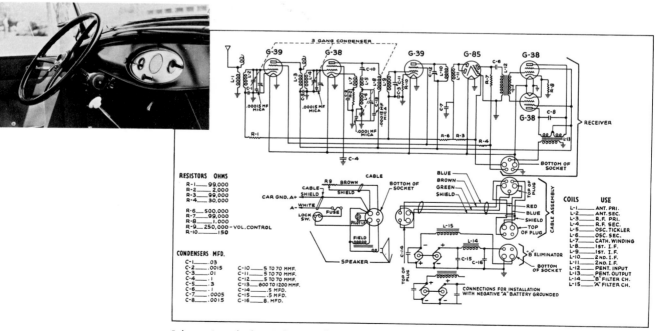

Schematic of the Police Radio version of the motor-generator set (commercial version schematic on page 62). This unit had tuneable frequency control, but only within the box at the set itself, and only the volume control, locking on/off switch, and pilot light were remoted.

In 1933 a new approach to radios in Ford cars was offered. This was the Glove Box radio in which the door and cardboard liner of the glove box were removed and this radio installed from the rear in their place. Self-contained and very excellent for its time, the glove box radio found limited favor however for it did mean the elimination of valuable storage space.

Ford Glove Box type radio as built by Zenith. Griggsby Grunow Co. also built a similar set, as well as one for Police use, but which was not a superhetrodyne set and therefore less powerful.

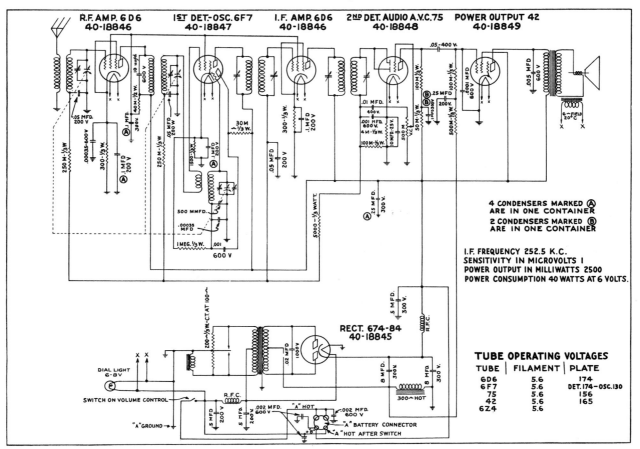

4 CONDENSERS MARKED Ⓐ ARE IN ONE CONTAINER
2 CONDENSERS MARKED Ⓑ ARE IN ONE CONTAINER

I.F. FREQUENCY 252.5 K.C.
SENSITIVITY IN MICROVOLTS 1
POWER OUTPUT IN MILLIWATTS 2500
POWER CONSUMPTION 40 WATTS AT 6 VOLTS.

TUBE OPERATING VOLTAGES

TUBE	FILAMENT	PLATE
6D6	5.6	174
6F7	5.6	DET. 174 — OSC. 130
75	5.6	156
42	5.6	165
6Z4	5.6	

In June of 1934, Ford introduced a new concept, the "Ford Center Control Radio" in which the controls were inserted in a styled "head" in place of the ash tray in the dash.

The essential portion of the '34 Center Control Radio is this container which holds all of the electronics including power supply and also speaker. It was installed under the dashboard in the space over the steering column where it was suspended upside down by two bolts through the cowl.

The 1935 radio itself is similar but was fitted with a control head more adaptable to the dashboard. The re-installation of the ashtray as shown is optional.

Control head of the '36 Center Control Radio is quite similar to that of 1935. However, trim of '35 is more nearly gray; that of '36 almost brown.

The radio on the far left is the '35/'36 style as seen from the tone control knob. Louvres, thought necessary for cooling in the '34 cabinet (at right) have been deleted. Both sets have a four pin test socket, but the later set also has a six pin receptacle for remoting the speaker and controls.

The Header Bar Speaker was introduced in February of 1935, and the speakers, in closed cars only, were installed in the header between the sun visors (see photo next page). Input power in all sets was supplied through a fused power lead wire.

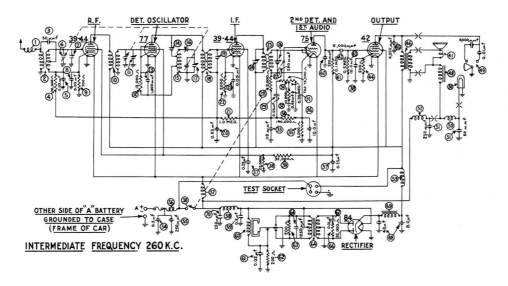

Schematic Drawing of 1935 Ford Auto Radio Receiver

The 1935 Header bar speaker (installed). This remote speaker was, at first, operated by a "center control" type radio in which the speaker had been eliminated and a blanking plate substituted. Later a more compact, rectanglar box was furnished (during 1936). Also, in 1936, a smaller speaker was employed which fit more conveniently behind a hole in the header trim plate allowing a flush header rather than this 1936 pertruding style.

1936 to 1939 Ford V-8 radios
(less speakers)

Although the control head on these radios could theoretically be used with the earlier style, such was not actually the case since the on/off switch had now been moved to the head and power to the set is controlled at that point. Earlier set had three-pin speaker remote cable; later on, in the 1939 set, a six pin receptacle was used.

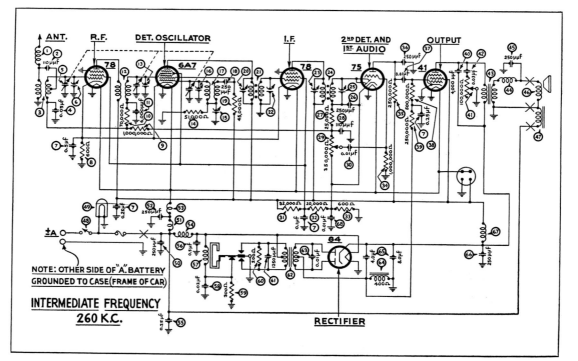

Schematic of late '36 box-type radio

Configuration of the earlier, sloped radio box continued for a time although when header bar speaker was employed, a blanking plate was used behind the speaker grill.

A 1938 radio in which the control head/speaker is piggy-backed to an earlier type box forming an essentially one-piece radio.

Popular accessory for the '35-'36 dashboard was the ashtray shown. Fully chromed, and with matching knob, it frequently was used in place of standard blanking plate or when radio was removed. Other styles include a rotating ashtray with V-8 trim which was genuine Ford accessory, as shown on page 270.

First of the *integral* behind-the-dash sets was this 1940 style. Built-in speaker mounts behind dashboard trim grill and controls protrude upwards through dash-board. Antenna feed is through connection behind the controls. Escutcheon plate is plastic (see next page).

'37 Dashboard had center control head installed above a pull-out ashtray, the lack of which in the '35-'36 was now corrected.

In 1938, a more permanent trend was established when the radio speaker, and its controls, was moved to the dashboard. Initially, a subassembly of the speaker and tuning controls was placed behind dash. Radio itself remained on the firewall.

(Dashboards illustrated at left, and below, do not have radios installed. The trim plates below the speaker grills would otherwise be removed to accommodate radio controls.)

The 1939 DeLuxe set was the first to incorporate push-button tuning. Several tunable capacitors were accessible from the bottom of the radio box and solenoid relay was used to place the set in either MANUAL or one of these pre-tuned modes.

The 1940 radio was the first in which entire radio was placed behind the dashboard. (Eliminated at this time was the windshield opening mechanism.) The radio had an unusual configuration including a "tunnel" for cowl ventilator mechanism. (Previous page.)

1941 Dashboard illustrating radio and controls.

STEERING

Steering wheels remained from the start at 17" diameter, but the lower end of the steering column changed several times. The three tooth "Worm & Sector" steering gear used from 1932-1936 was modified in 1935 from its earlier 13:1 ratio to 15:1 to provide better control.

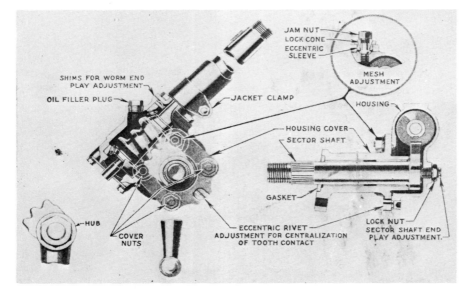

In 1936, and for that year only the Worm & Sector box was again modified, this time to provide needle bearings to reduce drag. Needle bearings were not again used in this application but the plain bushing-type of bearings returned with the next year's model.

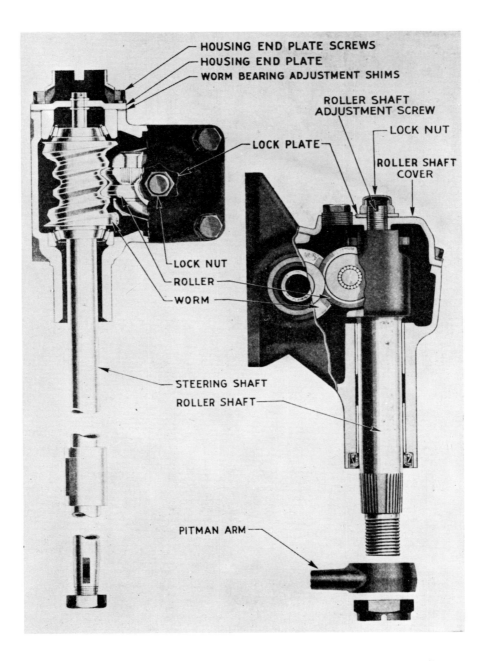

HOUSING END PLATE SCREWS
HOUSING END PLATE
WORM BEARING ADJUSTMENT SHIMS

ROLLER SHAFT
ADJUSTMENT SCREW

LOCK NUT

ROLLER SHAFT
COVER

LOCK PLATE

LOCK NUT
ROLLER
WORM

STEERING SHAFT
ROLLER SHAFT

PITMAN ARM

In 1937 the "Worm & Roller" type of steering box was introduced
which so greatly improved the steering
control that it has remained with us ever since.

This, a 1936 frame, shows the reinforcing cross members that added so greatly to the strength of the car. Early frame, in 1932, had no "X" members, and a greatly less rugged center cross member. All frames were made of 0.011 inch steel until 1934. Later was of .010″ except that the open car (and commercial) frames remained at 0.011 inches. Frame was lengthened in 1933, again in 1935, and for the last time, in 1941.

SPECIFICATIONS

1932-1942 FORD V-8 PASSENGER CAR BODY TYPES BY YEAR

	'32	'33	'34	'35	'36	'37	'38	'39	'40	'41	'42
Model No. (85 HP)	18	40	40	48	68	78	81-A	91-A	01A	11A	21A
(60 HP)						74	82-A	922-A	022A		

Body Type	'32	'33	'34	'35	'36	'37	'38	'39	'40	'41	'42
Fordor Sedan	━	━	━	━	━	━	━	━	━	━	━
Tudor Sedan	━	━	━	━	━	━	━	━	━	━	━
5—window Coupe	━	━	━	━	━	━	━	━	━	━	━
Club Coupe						━	━				
Sedan—Coupe											━
3—window Coupe	━	━	━	━							
Roadster	━	━	━	━	━	━					
Phaeton	━	━	━	━	━	━	━				
Cabriolet	━	━	━	━	━	━	━	━			
Convertible Club Coupe						━	━		━	━	━
Convertible Sedan	━			━	━	━	━	━			
Victoria	━	━	━								
Sport Coupe	━										
Sedan Delivery							━	━	━	◆	━
Station Wagon	◆	◆	◆	◆	◆	◆	━	━	━	━	━

◆ Listed as a commercial vehicle this year.

From 1932 through 1937, all cars were "standard" models although most were sold with "De Luxe" trim options, including cowl lamps and dual tail lights.

Commencing in 1938, "Standard", and "De Luxe" became distinct Lines.

In 1941, the lines expanded to SPECIAL (6 cylinder), DE LUXE (formerly the Standard), and SUPER DE LUXE (formerly the De Luxe).

The four crankshafts employed in the 85 and 95 HP engines

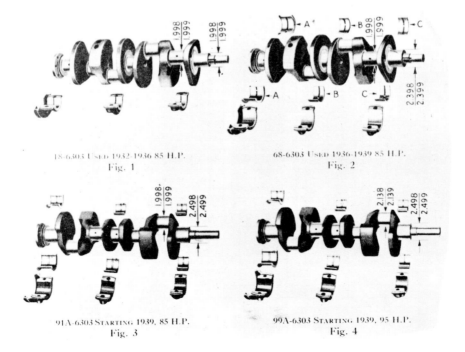

18-6303 Used 1932-1936 85 H.P.
Fig. 1

68-6303 Used 1936-1939 85 H.P.
Fig. 2

91A-6303 Starting 1939, 85 H.P.
Fig. 3

99A-6303 Starting 1939, 95 H.P.
Fig. 4

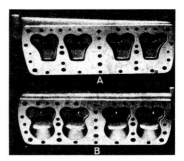

Both aluminum and also cast iron cylinder heads are used as shown (right). Also, flat-topped pistons were used prior to 1935. Photo at right shows type of combustion chamber used with flat top pistons (upper), and with domed-top (lower).

Ford V-8 Engine Specifications

Number of cylinders.............. 8
Type of block................. 90° V
Crankshaft degrees............. 90
Bore......................... 3.062
Stroke....................... 3.75"
Displacement cubic inches.......... 221
Taxable H.P. rating.............. 30.0
Firing order............1-5-4-8-6-3-7-2
Head "L" type

Lubrication

Pressure lubrication to all main bearings, connecting rod bearings and camshaft bearings.
Normal oil pressure at 2000 RPM 30 lbs. Oil pump 1.88 gallons per minute at 2000 RPM.

Oil capacity.................... 5 quarts
Type oil gauge................ Bayonette
Type oil pump.................. Gear
Drain plug diameter 1932 to 1938..... 0.75"
Starting 1939..................... 1.5"

Directed flow crankcase ventilation with outlet under the car starting 1935.

Cylinder Block
Ford cast alloy iron.
Water jackets full length of cylinders.
Offset of cylinders.............. 0.187"
Piston Pins
Float in rod and piston.
Retainer at ends of pin.
Diameter...............7501" to .7504"
Length steel piston................ 2.850"
Aluminum piston................ 2.780"
Clearance in steel piston........... .0005"
Fit in aluminum piston from .0001" tight to .0001" loose
Fit in rod .0001" loose.
Piston Rings
Top ring (compression) plain.
Width.................. .0915" to .0920"
Thickness............... .130" to .140"
Gap.................... .012" to .017"
No. 2 compression ring, 1932 to 1938 plain. 1939 to 1941 expander types.
Width.................. .0915" to .0920"
Thickness for steel pistons......108" to .112"
Thickness for aluminum pistons .096" to .100"
Gap........................ .012" to .017"

CYLINDER HEADS

Part Number		Material	Comp. Ratio	Max. Brake Horsepower		Maximum Torque		Compression Pressure			No. of Studs	Piston Type	Volume
								Maximum		At Cranking speed lbs.			
R.H.	L.H.			H.P.	R.P.M.	Lbs.	R.P.M.	Lbs.	R.P.M.				
18-6049	18-6050	Cast iron	5.5 to 1	85	3700	142	2200	130	2700	100	21	Flat	97-99 c.c.
40-6049A	40-6050A	Alum.	6.38 to 1	85	3800	148	2200	140	2700	113	21	Flat	58-61 c.c.
40-6049B	40-6050B	Cast iron	6.38 to 1	85	3800	148	2200	140	2700	113	21	Flat	79-81 c.c.
48-6049	48-6050	Alum.	6.38 to 1	85	3800	148	2200	140	2700	113	21	Dome	60 c.c.
68-6049	68-6050	Alum.	6.3 to 1	85	3800	148	2200	140	2700	112	21	Dome	60 c.c.
78-6050	78-6050	Alum.	6.2 to 1	85	3800	154	2200	140	2400	110	21	Dome	78 c.c.
77-6050	77-6050	Cast iron	7.5 to 1	94	3800	160	2200	165	2400	129	21	Dome	60-62 c.c.
81A-6049A	81A-6050A	Cast iron	6.2 to 1	90	3800	154	2200	145	2400	110	24	Dome	78-80 c.c.
81A-6049B	81A-6050B	Alum.	6.2 to 1	90	3800	154	2200	145	2400	110	24	Dome	78-80 c.c.
81T-6049	81T-6050	Cast iron	5.9 to 1	90	3800	154	2000	135	2300	108	24	Dome	83-85 c.c.
81AS-6049	81AS-6050	Cast iron	7.5 to 1	94	3800	160	2200	165	2400	129	24	Dome	60-62 c.c.
99AS-6049	99AS-6050	Cast iron	7.1 to 1	93	3800	160	2200	150	2400	124	24	Dome	65-67 c.c.
99T-6049	99T-6050	Cast iron	5.5 to 1	85	3700	154	2200	130	2400	100	24	Dome	90-92 c.c.
19AS-6049	19AS-6050	Cast iron	7.1 to 1	92	3800	160	2200	150	2400	124	24	Dome	70-72 c.c.

PISTONS

Part Number	Material	Dome	Skirt	Weight Grams	Fit of Piston in Cylinder (Using 0.50" Wide Feeler)			Ring Groove Width		
					Thickness of Blade		Pounds Pull on Feeler Blade	Top	Center	Bottom
					Hardened Sleeve Bore	Plain Bore				
40-6110-A to G	Aluminum	Flat	"T" slot	287-291	.0025"	.002"	6 to 10	.095"	.0945"	.1575"
68-6110-A & B	Steel	Spherical	Solid	304-308	.003"	.0025"	7 to 12	.095"	.0945"	.1575"
81A-6110-C to G	Aluminum	Spherical	"T" slot	304-308	.0025"	.002"	6 to 10	.095"	.0945"	.1575"
91A-6110-A & B	Steel	Spherical	Solid	333-337	.003"	.0025"	6 to 10	.095"	.0945"	.1575"
91A-6110-C to G	Aluminum	Spherical	"T" slot	333-337	.0025"	.002"	6 to 10	.095"	.0945"	.1575"

Oil Control Ring

1932 to 1938 plain oil control.
1938 to 1941 expander oil control.

Width 1932 to 1938	.1545" to .1550"
Width 1939 to 1941	.1535" to .1540"
Thickness for steel pistons	.108" to .112"
Thickness for alum. pistons	.096" to .100"
Gap	.012" to .017"

Connecting Rods

Length center to center	7.000"
Crankpin end bore	2.220"
Width crank pin end	.8725"
Bushing bore	.7505"
Bushing length	1.312"
Weight 1932 to 1936	471 grams
Weight 1937 to 1938	453 grams
Weight starting 1939	476 grams

Crankpin Bearing Inserts

Type floating.
Flanged 1932 to 1938. No flange starting 1939.
Two rods on each insert.

Length overall 1932 to 1938	1.933"
Length overall starting 1939	1.747"

Camshaft and Gear

Shaft material 1932 to 1934 forged steel starting 1935 special cast alloy steel.
Gear pressed on 1932 to 1940.
Gear bolted on starting 1940.
Gear material bakelized fabric 1932 to 1941 (aluminum partial production starting 1940).
Camshaft bearing 3 steel backed babbit lined.

Bearing diameter	1.797"
Length front	1.660"
Length center	1.400"
Length rear	1.776"

Crankshaft

Counter balanced 90 degree type.
Forged steel 1932 to 1934. Cast alloy steel starting 1935.

Length overall 1932 to 1938	24.47"
Length overall starting 1939	26.03"
Crank pin journal diameter	1.999"
Length 1932 to 1938	1.937"
Length starting 1939	1.75"

Main bearing journals diameter—

1932 to 1936	1.999"
1937 to 1938	2.399"
starting 1939	2.499"
Length front 1932 to 1938	1.841"
Length starting 1939	1.721"
Length center 1932 to 1938	1.736"
Length starting 1939	1.676"
Length rear	2.255"
Weight pounds 1932 to 1934	65.6 lbs.
Weight pounds 1935 to 1936	60. lbs.
Weight pounds 1937 to 1938	63.8 lbs.
Weight pounds starting 1939	66. lbs.
End play	.002" to .006"

Main bearing inserts length—

Front and center	1.506"
Rear	2.251"
Wall thickness	.0855"

Piloted cap no shims.

Flywheel and Starter Gear

Flywheel material cast iron.
Flywheel gear material steel.
Flywheel weight passenger car, 38.7 lbs., truck 34.1 lbs.

Valves

Mushroom stem.
Lifter non-adjustable hollow cast.
Valve, guide and spring removable as an assembly starting 1934.
Valve seat inserts (molybdenum chrome alloy steel) for exhaust 1933 to 1938, for both exhaust and intake starting 1939.
Valve material high chrome silicon alloy steel.

Diameter of head	1.537"
Diameter of stem	0.3115"
Diameter of stem end	0.550"
Diameter of seat angle	45 degrees
Diameter of lifter	0.9995"
Lift of cam	0.292"
Spring length valve closed	2.13"
Pressure valve closed	37 to 40 lbs.
Pressure valve open	76 to 80 lbs.
Stem clearance	.0015" to .0035"
Valve clearance	.011" to .012"

Valve timing	1932-36	1937-40
Intake opens B.T.C.	9.5°	0.0°
Intake closes A.B.C.	54.5°	44.0°
Exhaust opens B.B.C.	57.5°	48.0°
Exhaust closes A.T.C.	6.5°	6.0°

The "Thrifty Sixty" Ford 60 HP V-8 engine (1937-1940)

The two cranks employed in the 60 HP engine

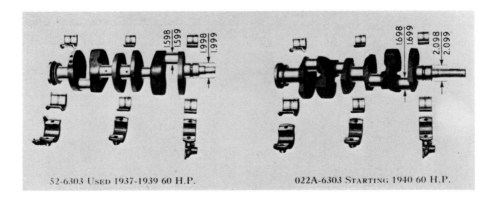

52-6303 Used 1937-1939 60 H.P.   022A-6303 Starting 1940 60 H.P.

FORD 60 HP V-8 ENGINE SPECIFICATIONS

Number of cylinders.................. 8
Type of block....................... 90°V
Crankshaft degrees.................. 90
Bore................................ 2.6"
Stroke.............................. 3.2"
Displacement cubic inches........... 136
Taxable H.P. rating................. 21.6
Firing order.............. 1-5-4-8-6-3-7-2
Head "L" type

Lubrication

Pressure lubrication to all mainbearings connecting rod bearings and camshaft bearings.

Normal oil pressure at 2000 RPM 30 lbs. Oil pump one gallon per minute at 2000 RPM.
Oil capacity.....................4 quarts
Type oil gauge................Bayonette
Type oil pump.....................Gear
Drain plug diameter................. 1.5"
Crankcase ventilation.

Cylinder Block

Ford cast alloy iron.
Water jackets full length of cylinders.
Offset of cylinders .... 0.141"

Piston Pins

Float in rod and piston retainer at ends of pin.
Diameter .... .6876" to .6879"
Length.......................... 2.368"
Clearance in steel piston .... .0004"
Fit in rod .0001" loose.

Piston Rings

Top ring (compression) plain
Width.................... .0920" to .0925"
Thickness...............115" to .120"
Gap.....................012" to .017"
No. 2 compression ring, 1937 to 1938 plain. 1939 to 1940 expander types.
Width.................... 0920" to .0925"
Thickness .... .098" to .102"
Gap.....................012" to .017"

CYLINDER HEADS

| Part Number | Material | Comp. Ratio | Max. Brake Horsepower | | Maximum Torque | | Compression Pressure | | | No. of Studs | Volume |
| | | | | | | | Maximum | | Pressure At Cranking Speed lbs. | | |
			H.P.	R.P.M.	Lbs.	R.P.M.	Lbs.	R.P.M.			
52-6050-B	Aluminum	6.6	60	3500	94	2500	158	2800	116	17	41-43 c.c.
52-6050-C	Cast Iron	6.6	60	3500	94	2500	158	2800	116	17	41-43 c.c.

PISTONS

| Part Number | Material | Dome | Skirt | Weight Grams | Fit of Piston in Cylinder (Using 0.50" Wide Feeler) | | | Ring Groove Width | | |
| | | | | | Thickness of Blade | | Pounds Pull on Feeler Blade | | | |
					Hardened Sleeve Bore	Plain Bore		Top	Center	Bottom
52-6110-A to F	Steel	Spherical	Solid	226-231	.0025"	.002"	7 to 12	.095"	.0945"	.1575"

Oil Control Ring

1937 to 1938 plain oil control.
1939 to 1941 expander oil control.

Width 1937 to 1938....... .1545" to .1550"
Width 1939 to 1940...... .1535" to .1540"
Thickness 1937-38........ .110" to .120"
Thickness 1939-40........ .094" to .098"
Gap................. .012" to .017"

Connecting Rods

Length center to center............ 6.125"
Crankpin end bore 1937 to 1939..... 1.800"
  1940................................ 1.900"
Width crank pin end............... .700"
Bushing Bore.................... .6879"
Bushing length.................. 1.115"
Weight 1937 to 1939............ 271 grams
Weight 1940................... 295 grams

Crankpin Bearing Inserts

Type floating.
    Flanged 1937 to 1939. No flange 1940.
    Two rods on each insert.
Length overall 1937 to 1939........ 1.535"
Length overall 1940............... 1.403"

Camshaft and Gear

Shaft material special cast alloy steel.
Gear pressed on.
Gear material bakelized fabric.
Camshaft bearing 3 steel backed babbit lined.
Bearing diameter.................. 1.498"
Length front..................... 1.2"
Length center................... 1.2"
Length rear..................... 1.0"

Crankshaft

Counter balanced 90 degree type.
Cast alloy steel.
Length overall 1937 to 1939........ 20.82"
Length overall 1940............... 22.88"
Crank pin journal diameter
  1937 to 1939.................. 1.599"
  1940......................... 1.699"
Length 1937 to 1939............. 1.54"
Length 1940.................... 1.408"

Main bearing journals diameter—

  1937 to 1939.................... 1.999"
  1940............................ 2.099"
Length front.................... 1.662"
Length center................... 1.648"
Length rear..................... 2.002"
Weight pounds 1937 to 1939...... 44.9 lbs.
Weight pounds 1940............. 40.5 lbs.
End play............... .002" to .005"
End play.............. .002 to .005 inch

Main bearing inserts length—

  front and center................ 1.510"
  rear............................ 1.999"
  wall thickness.................. .0855"
Piloted cap no shims.

Flywheel and Starter Gear

Flywheel material cast iron.
Flywheel gear material steel.
Flywheel weight 1937-39 passenger car, 31.3 lbs., commercial and 1940 passenger, 23.8 lbs.

Valves

Mushroom stem.
Lifter non-adjustable hollow cast.
Valve, guide and spring removable as an assembly.
Valve seat inserts (molybdenum chrome alloy steel) for exhaust.
Valve material high chrome silicon alloy steel.
Diameter of head................. 1.281"
Diameter of stem................. 0.2795"
Diameter of stem end............. 0.460"
Diameter of seat angle........ 45 degrees
Diameter of lifter................. 0.8295"
Lift of cam...................... 0.251"
Spring length valve closed........ 2.05"
Pressure valve closed........ 26 to 30 lbs.
Pressure valve open........... 48 to 52 lbs.
Stem clearance.......... .0015" to .0035"
Valve clearance........... .011" to .012"

Valve timing
Intake opens B.T.C................. 9.5°
Intake closes A.B.C............... 54.5°
Exhaust opens B.B.C.............. 57.5°
Exhaust closes A.T.C.............. 6.5°

Wheel and Tire Specifications
WHEELS

| | Wheel Pressed Steel | Type Steel Spoke | Rim | | Retainer Ring | | Diameter Bolt Circle | Number of Bolts |
			Size Inches	Drop Center	Split	Continuous		
1932.		Yes	18x3.25	Yes			5.5"	5
1933 and 1934.		Yes	17x3.25	Yes			5.5"	5
1935.		Yes	16x4.0	Yes			5.5"	5
1936-9 (85 H.P.).	Yes		16x4.0	Yes			10.25"	5
1937-9 (60 H.P.).	Yes		16x3.5	Yes			10.25"	5
Optional 1936-9.	Yes		18x3.62	Yes			10.25"	5
Starting 1940 (85 H.P.).	Yes		16x4.0	Yes			5.5"	5
Starting 1940 (60 H.P.).	Yes		16x3.5	Yes			5.5"	5

TIRES

	Tire Size	Plies	Inflation Pressure	Rim Width	Pounds Capac. Per Tire	Approximate Loaded Rolling Radius	Approximate Revolutions Per Mile	Road Clearance (Center of Rear Axle)
1932.	5.25x18"	4	35	3.25"	925	13.82"	723	9.0"
1933 and 1934.	5.50x17"	4	32	3.25"	955	13.68"	730	9.0"
Starting 1935—85 H.P.. . (Except Station Wagon)	6.00x16"	4	30	4.0"	915	13.38"	740	8.4"
Starting 1935—Station Wagon.	6.00x16"	6	36	4.0"	1065	13.46"	734	8.4"
Starting 1937—60 H.P.. .	5.50x16"	4	30	3.5"	810	12.8"	772	8.0"
Optional Starting 1936 Oversize.	6.50x16"	6	35	4.0"	1215	13.54"	730	8.7"
For extra road clearance.	6.00x18"	4	30	3.62"	1070	14.34"	696	9.5"
For extra road clearance.	6.00x18"	6	35	3.62"	1205	14.51"	688	9.7"

SERVICE BRAKES*

	Type of Brake	Brake Actuation	Diameter of Brake Drum		Brake Lining								Total Service Brake Area (Square Inches)
					Material#		Length Per Shoe		Width		Thickness		
			Front Wheels	Rear Wheels	Primary Shoe	Secondary Shoe	Front Wheel	Rear Wheel	Front Wheel	Rear Wheel	Front Wheel	Rear Wheel	
1932 to 1936	Non-Energ.	Rod	12"	12"	W	W	13.25"	13.25"	1.75"	1.75"	0.185"	0.185"	186
1937 and 1938	Energizing	Cable	12"	12"	M	W	13.25"	13.25"	1.75"	1.75"	0.185"	0.185"	186

	Type of Brake	Brake Actuation	Diameter of Hydraulic Wheel Cylinder Piston				Diameter of Master Cylinder	Diameter of Brake Drum		Brake Lining				Length Per Shoe				Width		Thickness		Total Service Brake Area (Square Inches)
			Front Wheel		Rear Wheel					Material#				Front Wheel		Rear Wheel		Front Wheel	Rear Wheel	Front Wheel	Rear Wheel	
			Forward Shoe	Reverse Shoe	Forward Shoe	Reverse Shoe		Front Wheel	Rear Wheel	Forward Shoe (Front)	Reverse Shoe (Front)	Forward Shoe (Rear)	Reverse Shoe (Rear)	Forward	Reverse	Forward	Reverse					
Starting 1939	Non-Energ.	Hydr.	1.25"	1.00"	1.125"	1.00"	1.062"	12"	12"	W	M			13.18"	10.1"	13.18"	10.1"	1.75"	1.75"	0.20"	0.20"	163

*All service brakes are four wheel, internal expanding with two shoes per wheel; drums cast alloy iron.

#Means M Molded. W means Woven.

HAND BRAKES

	Type of Brake	Brake Actuation	Diameter of Drum	Material		Brake Lining						Total Hand Brake Area (Sq. In.)	Service Brake Shoes Used for Hand Brake	Wheels Braked by Hand Brake
				Primary Shoe	Secondary Shoe	Length Per Wheel		Width		Thickness				
						Front	Rear	Front	Rear	Front	Rear			
1932 to 1936	Non-Energ.	Rod	12"	W	W	26.5"	26.5"	1.75"	1.75"	0.185"	0.185"	186	Yes	All
1937 and 1938	Energizing	Cable	12"	M	W	26.5"	26.5"	1.75"	1.75"	0.185"	0.185"	186	Yes	All

	Type of Brake	Brake Actuation	Drums		Hand Brake Lining			Total Hand Brake Area (Sq. In.)	Service Brake Shoes Used for Hand Brake	Wheels Braked by Hand Brake
			No.	Dia.	Material#	Width	Thickness			
Starting 1939	Non-Energ.	Cable	2	12"	M & W	1.75"	0.20"	81.5	Yes	Rear

Front Axle, Steering Gear and Alignment Specifications

FRONT AXLE* / STEERING GEAR

Year and Model	Taper Roller Wheel Bearings	Diameter inches	Bronze Bushings	Roller Thrust Bearing	Spindle Carrying Steering Arm	Radius Rods	Tread inches	Standard Wheelbase	101" Wheelbase	134" Wheelbase	157' or 158' Wheelbase	Worm and Roller	Worm and Sector	Tapered Roller on Worm Shaft	Needle Bearings	Plain Bushings	Worm End Play	Thrust Screw for Sector Shaft End Play	Mesh of Worm and Sector	Eccentric for Centralization of Tooth Contact	Gear Ratio	Steering Wheel Diameter inches
1932	2	0.812"	2	1	L	Yes	55¾"	19.5	—	—	—	No	Yes	2	No	2	Shims	Yes	Eccentric	Yes	13	17"
1933	2	0.812"	2	1	L	Yes	55¾"	20	—	—	—	No	Yes	2	No	2	Shims	Yes	Eccentric	Yes	13	17"
1934	2	0.812"	2	1	L	Yes	55¾"	20	—	—	—	No	Yes	2	No	2	Shims	Yes	Eccentric	Yes	15	17"
1935	2	0.812"	2	1	R	Yes	55¾"	20	—	—	—	No	Yes	2	No	2	No	Yes	Eccentric	Yes	15	17"
1936	2	0.812"	2	1	R	Yes	55¾"	20	—	—	—	No	Yes	2	2	No	No	Yes	Eccentric	Yes	17	17"
Starting 1937	2	0.812"	2	2 · 1	R	Yes	55¾"	19	—	—	—	Yes	—	2	No	2	Shims	No	Screw	No	18.2	17"

WHEEL ALIGNMENT

	CASTOR*		CAMBER#		Camber Plus Side Inclination		Toe-In†	TOE-OUT ON 20° TURN			
								Regular Wheelbase	Trucks Wheelbase		
	Max.	Min.	Max.	Min.	Max.	Min.			101"	134"	157" or 158"
1932	9°	4½°	1°	¼°	9°	8¼°	3/32"	23½°	—	—	—
1933 to 1935	9°	4½°	1°	¼°	9°	8¼°	3/32"	23⅓°	—	—	—
Starting 1936	9°	4½°	1°	¼°	9°	8¼°	1/16"	23⅓°	—	—	—

*Max. variation between wheels ½°. Limits shown are without load on vehicle.
#Max. variation between wheels ¼°. Camber of R. H. wheel should never be greater than L. H.
†Toe-in must be in proportion to camber. Use ratio of 1 to 10.

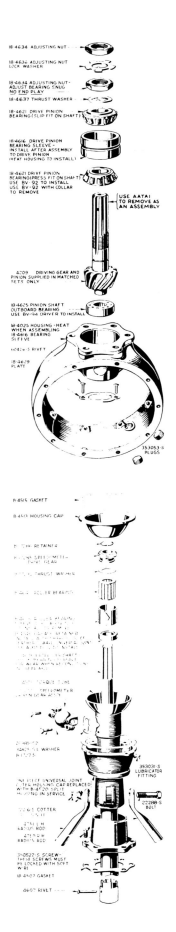

Rear Axle Specifications†

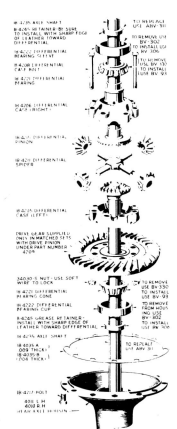

Year	Gear Ratio	Teeth Pinion	Teeth Gear	Tooth Back Lash	Pinion Bearing Adjustment Inch-Pounds	Axle Shaft Diameter	Tread with Std. Tires	Lubricant Capacity Pints	Type of Axle	Type of Gears	Drive Shaft	Type of Pinion Bearing Arrangement	Pinion Tapered Roller Bearings	Pinion Straight Roller Pilot Bearing	Differential Tapered Roller Bearings	Wheel Hub Number Per Wheel	Wheel Hub Type of Roller Bearing	No. of Drive Shaft Bearings (Straight Roller)
1932	Std. 4.11	9	37	.006-.010"	15-20	1.13"	58.25"	2.5 to 3	¾ Floating	Spiral bevel	Tubular	Spread	2	None	2	1	Straight	1
	Opt. 3.78	9	34															
1933 and 1934	Std. 4.11	9	37	.006-.010"	12-17	1.13"	58.25"	2.5 to 3	¾ Floating	Spiral bevel	Tubular	Straddle	2	1	2	1	Straight	1
	Opt. 4.33	9	39															
	Opt. 3.54	11	39																
1935 and 1936	Std. 4.11	9	37	.006-.010"	12-17	1.13"	58.25"	2.5 to 3	¾ Floating	Spiral bevel	Tubular	Straddle	2	1	2	1	Straight	1
	Opt. 4.33	9	39																
	Opt. 3.78	9	34																
	Opt. 3.54	11	39																
1937 to 1940 85 H.P.	Std. 3.78	9	34	.012" Max	12-17	1.13"	58.25"	2.5 to 3	¾ Floating	Spiral bevel	Solid	Straddle	2	1	2	1	Straight	2
	Opt. 3.54	11	39																
	Opt. 4.11	9	37																
60 H.P. (except Comm. 1940)	Std. 4.44	9	40	.012" Max	12-17	1.13"	58.25"	2.5 to 3	¾ Floating	Spiral bevel	Solid	Straddle	2	1	2	1	Straight	2
60 H.P. Comm. (1940)	Std. 4.55	9	41	.012" Max	12-17	1.13"	58.25"	2.5 to 3	¾ Floating	Spiral bevel	Solid	Straddle	2	1	2	1	Straight	2

†All rear axles are torque tube drive with radius rods

SPRINGS

	Front								Rear					
	Number	Type	Strut Rod	Ride Stabilizer	Spring Covers	Mounted Ahead of Front Axle	Leaves Lubricated Through Tie Bolt	Oilless Shackles	Number	Type	Spring Covers	Mounted Behind Rear Axle	Leaves Lubricated Through Tie Bolt	Oilless Shackles
1932 to 1934..	1	Transverse	No	No	No	No	No	Yes	1	Transverse	No	Yes	No	Yes
1935 and 1936.	1	Transverse	No	No	No	Yes	No	Yes	1	Transverse	No	Yes	No	Yes
1937 to 1939..	1	Transverse	No	No	No	Yes	Yes	Yes	1	Transverse	No	Yes	Yes	Yes
1940........	1	Transverse	No	†Yes	□No	Yes	Yes	Yes	1	Transverse	□No	Yes	Yes	Yes

†No ride stabilizer used on 60 H.P. units.

	Front					Rear				
	Part Number	Length Eye to Eye Loaded	Width	No. of Lves.	Load Rate*	Part Number	Length Eye to Eye Loaded	Width	No. of Lves.	Load Rate*
1932	40-5310-C	32.6″	1.75″	12	400	40-5560-J	46.0″	2.25″	11†	230
1933-34	40-5310-C	32.6″	1.75″	12	400	40-5560-F	46.0″	2.25″	11†	225
1935-36	78-5310-C	40.3″	2.0″	11	245	78-5560-B	46.6″	2.25″	11†	180
1937 {85 H.P.	78-5310-C	40.3″	2.0″	11	245	78-5560-B	46.6″	2.25″	11†	180
60 H.P.	74-5310-B	40.3″	2.0″	10	215	78-5560-B	46.6″	2.25″	11†	180
1938 and {85 H.P.	78-5310-C	40.3″	2.0″	11	245	78-5560-B	46.5″	2.25″	11†	180
1939 {60 H.P.	74-5310-B	40.3″	2.0″	10	215	78-5560-A	46.5″	2.25″	10†	165
1940 {85 H.P.	01A-5310-B†	41.8″	2.0″	10	185	01A-5560-C	46.5″	2.25″	10†	165
{60 H.P.	022A-5310-A†	40.3″	2.0″	10	215	01A-5560-C	46.5″	2.25″	10†	165

Other Springs

	Front					Rear				
	Part Number	Length Eye to Eye Loaded	Width	No. of Lves.	Load Rate*	Part Number	Length Eye to Eye Loaded	Width	No. of Lves.	Load Rate*
1932 to 34	40-5310-C	32.6″	1.75″	12	400	B-5560-A	45.9″	2.25″	10	210
						B-5560-B	45.9″	2.25″	9	180
						B-5560-C	46.0″	2.25″	9	155
						40-5560-G	46.0″	2.25″	10	200
						40-5560-H	46.0″	2.25″	12	240
						40-5560-J	46.0″	2.25″	11	230
						40-5560-K	46.0″	2.25″	13	330
						40-5560-L	46.0″	2.25″	12	250
Starting 1935	78-5310-D	40.3″	2.0″	12	305	78-5560-C	46.5″	2.25″	12	215
	78-5310-E	40.3″	2.0″	13	325	78-5560-D	46.8″	2.25″	14	330
						78-5560-E	46.6″	2.25″	13	245
						78-5560-F	46.8″	2.25″	15	375
						78-5560-G	46.5″	2.25″	9	155
Starting 1940	01A-5310-D	41.9″	2.0″	11	200	01A-5560-A	46.3″	2.25″	8	140
	01A-5310-F	41.9″	2.0″	12	240	01A-5560-B	46.5″	2.25″	9	155
						01A-5560-G	46.8″	2.25″	14	330
	022A-5310-B	40.3″	2.0″	11	245	01A-5560-E	46.5″	2.25″	12	215

*Figures shown are pounds per inch deflection per spring.

FRAME

	"X" Member	Box Type Center Cross Member	Channels Full Length of Frame	SIDE CHANNELS			
				Length	Depth (Max.)	Flange Width (Max.)	Thickness
1932............................	No	No	2	148.4″	6.0″	2.0″	0.11″
1933 and 1934....................	Yes	Yes	4	149.7″	6.0″	1.76″	0.11″
1935 to 1940....................	Yes	Yes	4	157.3″	5.5″	2.0″	*0.10″

*Thickness is 0.11″ for commercial and open passenger types.

Transmission, Clutch and Universal Joint Specifications

TRANSMISSION

	Transmission Cluster Gear Number	Forward Speeds	Type of Gears: Second Speed	Type of Gears: Other Speeds (Forward and Reverse)	Constant Mesh Second Speed Gear	Synchronizer for High and Second	Blocker Type Synchronizer	Main Drive Gear	Main Splined Shaft: Front End (Pilot)	Main Splined Shaft: Rear Bearing	Bearings Number	Cluster Gear: Type	Reverse Idler Gear	First (Low)	Second	Third (High on Car)	Fourth	Reverse	Lubricant Capacity (Pts.)	Location of Gear Shift Lever
Ford Passenger 85 H. P.																				
1932 to 1935..	48-7113	3	Helical	Spur	Yes	Yes	No	Ball	Roller	Ball	2	Roller	Bushing	2.82	1.604	1.0	None	3.383	2.5	Floor
1936 to 1939..	68-7113-A	3	Helical	Helical	Yes	Yes	No	Ball	Roller	Ball	2	Roller	Bushing	2.82	1.604	1.0	None	3.625	2.5	Floor
1940........	68-7113-A	3	Helical	Helical	Yes	Yes	Yes	Ball	Roller	Ball	2	Roller	Bushing	2.82	1.604	1.0	None	3.625	2.75	Steering Column
Ford Passenger 60 H. P.																				
1937......	74-7113-A	3	Helical	Spur	Yes	Yes	No	Ball	Roller	Ball	2	Bushings	Bushing	3.071	1.765	1.0	None	4.015	1.75	Floor
1938 & 1939..	74-7113-D	3	Helical	Helical	Yes	Yes	No	Ball	Roller	Ball	2	Bushings	Bushing	3.070	1.832	1.0	None	4.015	1.75	Floor
1940........	022A-7113-A	3	Helical	Helical	Yes	Yes	Yes	Ball	Roller	Ball	2	Bushings	Bushing	3.114	1.773	1.0	None	4.001	2.75	Steering Column

CLUTCH†

UNIVERSAL JOINTS#

	Pressure Increased by Centrifugal Force	Vibration Dampener in Hub Spring Type	Cushion Spring Type Clutch Disc	Throwout Bearing: Type	Throwout Bearing: Lubrication	Pilot Bearing: Type	Pilot Bearing: Lubrication	Total Clutch Pressure with Idling Engine (pounds)	Total Clutch Pressure at 4000 R.P.M. (pounds)	Clutch Facings: Outside Diameter	Clutch Facings: Inside Diameter	Clutch Facings: Facing Thickness	Clutch Facings: Friction Area (sq. in.)	Clutch Pedal Free Travel	Universal Joints: Number Used	Universal Joints: Type of Bearing in Joint
Ford Passenger and Commercial 85 H. P.																
1932 to 1934..	No	No	No	Ball	Cup	Ball	Pre-lub.	1140	1140	9.0"	5.76"	0.140"	75.1	.75—1.0"	1	Bushings
1935 to 1937..	Yes	Yes	Yes	Ball	Pre-lub.	Ball	Pre-lub.	810	1980	9.0"	5.76"	0.140"	75.1	1.5—1.75"	1	Bushings
1938 and 1939	Yes	Yes	Yes	Ball	Pre-lub.	Ball	Pre-lub.	810	1685	9.0"	5.76"	0.137"	75.1	1.5—1.75"	1	Bushings
1940........	Yes	Yes	Yes	Ball	Pre-lub.	Ball	Pre-lub.	810	1685	9.0"	5.76"	0.137"	75.1	1.0—1.25"	1	Bushings
Ford Passenger 60 H. P.																
1937 to 1939..	No	No	No	Ball	Pre-lub.	Ball	Pre-lub.	810	810	8.5"	6.0"	0.125"	56.94	.75—1.0"	1	Bushings
1940........	Yes	Yes	Yes	Ball	Pre-lub.	Ball	Pre-lub.	810	1685	9.0"	5.76"	0.137"	75.1	1.0—1.25"	1	Bushings
Ford Commercial 60 H. P.																
1937......	Yes	Yes	Yes	Ball	Pre-lub.	Ball	Pre-lub.	810	1980	9.0"	5.76"	0.140"	75.1	1.5—1.75"	1	Bushings
1938 and 1939	Yes	Yes	Yes	Ball	Pre-lub.	Ball	Pre-lub.	810	1685	9.0"	5.76"	0.137"	75.1	1.5—1.75"	1	Bushings
1940........	Yes	Yes	Yes	Ball	Pre-lub.	Ball	Pre-lub.	810	1685	9.0"	5.76"	0.137"	75.1	1.0—1.25"	1	Bushings

†All clutches are dry single plate.

Cooling System Specifications

	Thermostatic Control of Circulation	Location of Thermostats	Location of Water Pumps	Location of Fan	BELT DRIVES		
					Fan	Gener- ator	Water Pumps
1932 and 1933..	No	None	Heads	Generator Shaft	Yes	Yes	Yes
1934 to 1936...	Yes	Upper Hoses	Heads	Generator Shaft	Yes	Yes	Yes
1937 to 1939...	Yes	Heads	Block	Generator Shaft#	Yes#	Yes	Yes
1940.........	Yes	Heads	Block	Crankshaft	No	Yes	Yes

#DeLuxe 1939 has fan mounted on front end of crankshaft.

	Capacity of Cooling System Quarts	Pump Capacity Gal. per Min. at 3000 RPM	No. of Fan Blades	Fan Diameter	Effective Core Frontal Area Sq.In.	Hose Inside Diameter	BELT*	
							Approx. Inside Length	Part Number
1932......	22	25	4	15.5"	374	1.75"	51.2"	18-8620
1933 & 1934	22	25	4	15.5"	386	1.75"	54.06"	40-8620
1935.....	20	25	4	15.5"	382.5	1.75"	54.06"	40-8620
1936.....	22	25	4	15.5"	391	1.75"	54.06"	40-8620
1937 & 1938								
85 HP..	22	45	4	15.75"	362	1.75"	51.3"	78-8620A
60 HP..	15	20	4	15.75"	341	1.5"	43.9"	52-8620C
1939								
DeL. 85 HP	22	45	6	{3 blades 16.75"} {3 blades 14.75"}	384	1.75"	50.1"	78-8620B
85 HP	22	45	4	15.75"	362	1.75"	51.3"	78-8620A
60 HP	15	20	4	15.75"	341	1.5"	43.9"	52-8620C
1940								
85 HP..	22	45	6	{3 blades 16.75"} {3 blades 14.75"}	384	1.75"	51.3"	78-8620A
60 HP..	13	20	2	14.8"	384	1.5"	43.9"	52-8620C

*All belts are .63" wide max. Pulley groove angle is 28°.

FUEL TANK CAPACITY

1932 . . . . 10 gallons

1933/34 (except Victoria) . . . . 11 gallons

1933/34 Victoria . . . . 14 gallons

1935/40 (except '40 sedan delivery) . . . . 14 gallons

1940 Sedan Delivery . . . . 17 gallons

1941/42 . . . . 17 gallons

BATTERY

Year	Ford Deluxe	Ford Pass.	Optional Batteries		
1932	18-10655	18-10655	B-10655-B		
1933	40-10655A	40-10655A			
1934	40-10655-C	40-10655-C	91AS-10655B		
1935	40-10655-C	40-10655-C	91AS-10655B		
1936	40-10655-C	40-10655-C	91AS-10655B	40-10655-D	
1937	78-10655A	78-10655-A	78-10655B	81AS-10655	
1938	81A-10655A	81A-10655A	91AS-10655-B	81A-10655-B	81AS-10655
1939	81A-10655A	81A-10655A	91AS-10655-B	81A-10655-B	81AS-10655
1940	01A-10655A	01A-10655A			

Part Number	Volts	Located Under	Plates Per Cell	Dimensions			Capacity (any 3 cells)			Total Plate Area (Sq. In.)	Type Filler	Bench Charging Rate Amperes	
				Height	Width	Length	Ampere Hours (20 Hour Rate)	Amperes (20 Minute Rate)	Minutes at 0°F. with 300 Amp. Discharge			Start	Finish
B-10655-B	6	Floor	15	7.8"	7.1"	9.15"	95	120	3.00	2496	Plain	6	4
18-10655	6	Floor	13	7.8"	7.1"	9.15"	82	103	2.20	2163	Plain	6	4
40-10655-C	6	Floor	17	7.1"	7.2"	10.5"	100	126	3.30	2559	Plain	8	5
40-10655-D	6	Floor	15	7.1"	7.2"	10.5"	90	110	2.35	2258	Plain	6	4
78-10655-A	6	Hood	17	7.1"	7.2"	10.5"	100	126	3.30	2559	Vent Hose	8	5
78-10655-B	6	Hood	15	7.1"	7.2"	10.5"	90	110	2.35	2258	Vent Hose	6	4
81A-10655-A	6	Hood	17	7.1"	7.2"	10.5"	100	126	3.30	2559	Bellows	8	5
81A-10655-B	6	Either	15	7.1"	7.2"	10.5"	90	110	2.35	2258	Bellows	6	4
81AS-10655	6	Hood	19	8.9"	7.2"	10.5"	135	170	4.45	3505	Plain	10	8
81B-10655	12	Floor	13	10.0"	11.0"	21.2"	133	140	3.7	5712	Plain	8	5
86H-10655	6	Either	17	7.1"	7.2"	10.5"	100	126	3.30	2559	Bellows	8	5
91AS-10655-B	6	Either	11	7.9"	7.2"	10.5"	65	63	2.0	1656	Plain	6	4
01A-10655-A	6	Hood	17	9.2"	7.3"	10.6"	120	150	4.0	3043	Bellows	10	8
06H-10655-A	6	Hood	17	9.2"	7.3"	10.6"	120	150	4.0	3043	Bellows	10	8
09B-10655	12	Floor	17	9.8"	10.9"	20.5"	158	215	5.1	8172	Plain	15	10
9DT-10655	12	Floor	25	10.0"	11.0"	21.2"	180	215	2.2	4128	Plain	15	10
SE51-10655	12	Floor	15	9.8"	9.8"	20.5"	137	150	2.8	5040	Plain	15	10

NOTE: "81A" Batteries can be placed in cars where battery is under floor, seat or hood.
"40" Batteries can only be used in cars where battery is under floor or seat.
"78" Batteries can only be used under hood as the vent hose type filler plugs require extra head clearance.

Generator Specifications

Part Number	Pulley "O.D." in Inches	Watts	CHARACTERISTICS — Engine R.P.M. Charge Starts	CHARACTERISTICS — Maximum Rate Amps.	CHARACTERISTICS — Maximum Rate Engine R.P.M.	Amps. at 3000 R.P.M.	BRUSHES	FIELD Part Number	FIELD Ohms at 70° F.	FIELD Ohms at 140° F.	ARMATURE Part Number	ARMATURE Ohms at 70° F.	ARMATURE Ohms at 140° F.	Generator Replaced in Service by Part Number
B-10000	3.62						3	40-10175	1.0	1.22	46-10005	.29	.36	
BB-10000-D	3.68	119	500	17	1300	11	3	40-10175	1.0	1.22	18-10005	.29	.36	82A-10000-A
18-10000-A	4.08	189	1000	27	1300	11	3	40-10175	1.0	1.22	18-10005	.29	.36	
18-10000-H	4.08						3	40-10175-H	1.44	1.75	18-10005-H	.41	.50	
40-10000-A	4.08	119	500	17	1300	11	3	40-10175	1.0	1.22	18-10005	.29	.36	81A-10000-A
40-10000-B	4.38						3	40-10175	1.0	1.22	18-10005	.29	.36	81A-10000-A
40-10000-H	4.40						3	40-10175-H	1.44	1.75	18-10005-H	.41	.50	81A-10000-B
46-10000-H	3.62						3	40-10175	1.0	1.22	46-10005	.29	.36	B-10000
46-10000-B	4.08*						3	40-10175	1.0	1.22	18-10005	.29	.36	79-10000-B
51-10000-A	5.18	119	500	17	1300	11	3	40-10175	1.0	1.22	18-10005	.29	.36	81A-10000-A
67-10000-A	5.18	182	525	26	1250	16	3	40-10175-H	1.44	1.75	68-10005-H	.19	.23	81A-10000-B
67-10000-H	4.38	182	525	26	1000	16	3	40-10175	1.0	1.22	18-10005	.29	.36	81A-10000-A
68-10000-A	4.38	182	525	26	1250	16	3	68-10175-H	1.44	1.75	68-10005-H	.19	.23	81A-10000-B
68-10000-HA	4.38	126	350	18	1000	16	3	68-10175-H	1.44	1.75	18-10005	.29	.36	82A-10000-C
68-10000-HB	3.68	126	350	18	950	16	3	68-10175-H	1.44	1.75	18-10005	.29	.36	82A-10000-B
74-10000-HA	3.68	126	350	18	1200	16	3	68-10175-H	1.44	1.75	74-10005-HA	.19	.32	81A-10000-D
74-10000-HB	4.38	182	500	26	1200	16	3	68-10175-H	1.44	1.75	74-10005-HB	.19	.36	81A-10000-E
78-10000-A	4.38	196	525	28	1250	16	3	78-10175	2.7	3.3	78-10005-A	.19	.23	81A-10000-B
78-10000-B	4.38	182	525	26	1250	16	3	78-10175	2.7	3.3	78-10005-B	.29	.36	82A-10000-B
78-10000-HA	3.68	126	350	18	1000	16	3	68-10175-H	1.44	1.75	78-10005-HA	.19	.23	81A-10000-E
78-10000-HB	4.38	126	350	18	1000	16	3	68-10175-H	1.44	1.75	78-10005-HA	.19	.23	
78-10000-HC	4.68*	126	350	18	1000	16	3	68-10175-H	1.44	1.75	78-10005-HB	.29	.36	
79-10000-B	4.68*	119	500	17	1350	11	3	40-10175	1.0	1.22	79-10005-A	.19	.23	
79-10000-HA	4.68*	182	525	26	1300	16	3	78-10175-H	1.44	1.75	79-10005-HA	.19	.23	81T-10000-A
79-10000-HB	4.38	126	525	18	850	16	3	78-10175-H	1.44	1.75	79-10005-HB	.29	.36	81T-10000-B
81A-10000-A	4.38	119	500	17	1300	11	3	40-10175	1.0	1.22	79-10005-A	.19	.23	
81A-10000-B	4.38	182	525	26	1250	16	3	78-10175-H	1.44	1.75	79-10005-HA	.19	.23	
81A-10000-C	4.38	126	350	18	1000	16	3	78-10175-H	1.44	1.75	79-10005-HB	.29	.36	81A-10000-E
81A-10000-D	4.38	196	500	28	1250	28	2	78-10175	2.7	3.3	79-10005-A	.19	.23	
81A-10000-E	4.68*	140	350	20	1000	20	2	78-10175	2.7	3.3	78-10005-A	.18	.20	
81T-10000-A	4.68*	196	550	28	1300	28	2	78-10175	2.7	3.3	78-10005-B	.29	.36	
81T-10000-B	4.68*	140	350	20	1050	20	2	78-10175	2.7	3.3	78-10005-A	.18	.20	
82A-10000-A	3.71	119	500	17	1300	11	3	40-10175	1.0	1.22	79-10005-A	.19	.23	82A-10000-D
82A-10000-B	3.71	182	525	26	1250	16	3	78-10175-H	1.44	1.75	82A-10005-A	.19	.23	82A-10000-E
82A-10000-C	3.71	126	350	18	1000	16	3	78-10175-H	1.44	1.75	82A-10005-B	.29	.36	
82A-10000-D	3.68	196	500	28	1250	28	2	78-10175	2.7	3.3	78-10005-A	.18	.20	
82A-10000-E	3.68	140	350	20	1000	20	2	78-10175	2.7	3.3	78-10005-B	.29	.36	
91A-10000	3.68	196	500	28	1250	28	4	78-10175	2.7	3.3	78-10005-A	.18	.20	
99B-10000	4.68†	500	720	55	1150	55	4	99B-10175	5.44	6.4	99B-10005	.06	.08	
01A-10000	3.68	222	400	32	1100	32	2	01A-10175	2.1	2.5	01A-10005	.16	.18	
01AS-10000-A	4.26						4	01AS-10175	4.0	4.65	99B-10005	.06	.08	
01AS-10000-B	3.68						4	01AS-10175	4.0	4.65	99B-10005	.06	.08	
01TS-10000	4.26						4	99B-10175	5.44	6.4	99B-10005	.06	.08	

*Double. †Triple.

Starter and Ignition Specifications

STARTER MOTOR

	Normal Engine Cranking Speed	Maximum Torque		Teeth in Pinion	Teeth in Ring Gear	Gear Ratio
		Pound-Feet	Load (Amps.)			
1932 to 1936.........	100	14	500	10	112	11.2
1937 to 1940						
85 HP and 95 HP..	100	14	500	10	112	11.2
60 HP..........	100	14	500	9	122	13.6

DISTRIBUTOR

Single unit with ignition coil in single waterproof housing; driven direct from front end of camshaft; spark advance fully automatic with vacuum controlled centrifugal governor; two sets of breaker points.

Adjustments: Initial spark advance; vacuum brake control; breaker point gap;

	Initial Spark Advance (Deg. on Crankshaft)	Automatic Advance over Initial (Deg. on Crankshaft)	Automatic Advance		Resistance of Primary Ignition Circuit (Ohms)	Number of Ignition Coils	Number of Pairs of Firing Points	Breaker Spring Tension (Ozs.)	Breaker Point Gap
			Begins (RPM)	Ends (RPM)					
1932........	4	16	400	3000	1.0-1.33	1	1	19-22*	.012"-.014"
1933........	4	22	400	3000	1.0-1.33	1	1	19-22*	.012"-.014"
1934 to 1936..	4	16	400	3000	1.0-1.33	1	1	22-27	.012"-.014"
1937 to 1940..	4	16	400	3000	1.0-1.33	1	1	20-24	.014"-.016"

*Tension should be 22-27 ounces when the larger diameter breaker points (same as 1934 to 1936 cars) are used.

SPARK PLUGS

	Thread	Make	Type	Gap
1932.....................	7/8"	Champion		.025"
1933.....................	18 M.M.	Champion	C-7	.025"
1934—Standard...........	18 M.M.	Champion	7	.025"
Optional (Cold plug)...........	18 M.M.	Champion	6 Com.	.020"
1935 to 1937—85 HP........	18 M.M.	Champion	7	.025"
1937—60 HP..............	14 M.M.	Champion	H-10	.025"
1938 to 1940, all engines......	14 M.M.	Champion	H-10	.025"

Light and Horn Specifications

LIGHTS

Year and Model	Bulb Type	Watts Each Country Beam	Inches Height Empty	Inches from Center of Car	Switch Location	Separate Beam Control Located	Beam Indicator Bulb	Fuse Amps.	Circuit Breaker	Parking Bulbs C.P.	Tail Light Bulbs C.P.	Stop Light Bulbs C.P.	Inside Body Lt. Bulbs C.P.	Instr. Panel Bulbs C.P.
1932														
Ford Car	32-32	27	38	14	Steering Wheel	—	No	20	No	3	3	21	3	3
1933														
Ford Car 5-Pass.	32-32	27	29¼†	16½	Steering Wheel	—	No	20	No	3	3	21	3	3
Ford 3-Pass.	32-32	27	32¼	16½	Steering Wheel	—	No	20	No	3	3	21	3	3
1934														
Ford Car 5-Pass.	32-32	27	29¼†	16½	Steering Wheel	—	No	20	No	3	3	21	3	3
Ford 3-Pass.	32-32	27	32¼	16½	Steering Wheel	—	No	20	No	3	3	21	3	3
1935														
Ford Car 5-Pass.	32-32	27	31½†	17⅜	Steering Wheel	—	No	20	No	3	3	21	3	3
Ford 3-Pass.	32-32	27	33½	17⅜	Steering Wheel	—	No	20	No	3	3	21	3	3
1936														
Ford Car 5-Pass.	32-32	27	31½†	16½	Steering Wheel	—	No	20	No	3	3	21	3	3
Ford 3-Pass.	32-32	27	33½	16½	Steering Wheel	—	No	20	No	3	3	21	3	3
1937														
Ford Car	32-32	27	30½	16½	Steering Wheel	—	No	20	No	1.5	3	21	3	3
1938														
Ford Car	32-32	27	30½	16½	Steering Wheel	—	No	20	No	1.5	3	21	3	3
1939														
Ford Car	32-32	27	30½	24	Steering Wheel	Floor	1.0	No	Vibrator	1.5*	3	21	3	3
1940														
Ford Car	Sealed	45-35	30½	24	Dash	Floor	1.0	No	Yes	1.5*	3	21	3	1.0

297

HORNS

Year and Model	No. of Horns	Type	Amperes Total

1932

Ford Deluxe Cars	1	Vibrator	6 to 8
All other types	1	Vibrator	6 to 8

1933

Ford Deluxe Cars	2	Vibrator	12 to 16
All other types	1	Vibrator	6 to 8

1934

Ford Deluxe Cars	2	Vibrator	12 to 16
All other types	1	Vibrator	6 to 8

1935

Ford Deluxe Cars	2	Vibrator	12 to 16
All other types	1	Vibrator	6 to 8

1936

Ford Deluxe Cars	2	Vibrator	12 to 16
All other Ford types	1	Vibrator	6 to 8

1937

Ford Deluxe Cars	2	Vibrator	12 to 16
All other Ford types	1	Vibrator	6 to 8

1938

Ford Deluxe Cars	2	Air Electric	24 to 28
All other Ford types	1	Vibrator	6 to 8

1939

Ford Passenger Cars	2	Air Electric	24 to 28
Commercial Cars	1	Vibrator	6 to 8

1940

Ford Passenger Cars	2	Air Electric	24 to 28
Commercial Cars	1	Vibrator	6 to 8

Window Glass Sizes (before cutting)

1932

ROADSTER—Standard & DeLuxe, Models B & 18.
Type B-40.

PHAETON--Standard & DeLuxe, Models B & 18.
Type B-35.

Windshield	12x44
*Back ($19\frac{11}{16}$x6) ($1\frac{1}{8}$" R. Cors.)	6x20

COUPE—Standard. 2-P. Models B & 18.
Type B-45.

Windshield	14x44
Door	16x24
Quarter	12x14
Note: Two Different Sized Back Lights.	
Back (With Rumble Seat)	12x26
Back (Without Rumble Seat)	10x26

COUPE—Sport. Rumble Seat. 2-4P. Models B & 18.
Type B-50. 4 and 8-Cyl.

Windshield	14x44
Door	14x34
*Back ($19\frac{11}{16}$x6) ($1\frac{1}{8}$" R. Cors.)	6x20

COUPE—DeLuxe. 2-P. Models B & 18.
Type B-520.

Windshield	12x44
Door	14x34
Back	10x32

CABRIOLET—2-4P. Models B & 18.
Type B-68.

Windshield	12x44
Door	16x26
*Back (22-27/32x$3\frac{15}{16}$) ($1\frac{3}{8}$" R. Cors.)	4x24

TUDOR SEDAN—2-D. Standard, DeLuxe. Models B & 18.
Type B-55. 4 and 8-Cyl.

Windshield	14x44
Door	16x32
Quarter	16x32
Back	10x26

FORDOR SEDAN—4-D. Standard, DeLuxe, Model B.
Type B-160. 4 and 8-Cyl.

Windshield	14x44
Front Door	16x24
Rear Door	16x26
Quarter	16x16
Back	10x26

VICTORIA—2D-4P. Models B & 18.
Type B-190.

Windshield	14x44
Door	14x32
Quarter	14x22
Back	10x26

SEDAN—Convertible. 2D. Models B & 18.
Type B-400.

Windshield	12x44
Door	14x32
Quarter	14x20
*Back ($19\frac{11}{16}$x6) ($1\frac{1}{8}$" R. Cors.)	6x20

*Cut to Size. No Pattern Required.

1933

CABRIOLET—2-4P. Models 40, 46., 4-Cyl. V-8.

Windshield	14x42
Door	14x32
*Back ($23\frac{7}{8}$x$3\frac{15}{16}$) (1" R. Cors.)	4x24

TUDOR SEDAN—2D-5P. Models 40, 46.
Type 700.

VICTORIA—2D-5P. Models 40
Type 740.

Windshield	14x42
Door	16x34
Quarter (Victoria)	16x24
Quarter (Tudor Sedan)	16x34
Back	10x32

FORDOR SEDAN—4D-5P. Models 40
Type 730.

Windshield	14x42
Front Door	16x28
Rear Door	16x26
Quarter	16x16
Back	10x32

ROADSTER—2-4P. and Sport 2-4P. Models 40,

Windshield	12x44
*Back ($23\frac{3}{4}$x$3\frac{15}{16}$) ($1\frac{3}{8}$" R. Cors.)	4x24

COUPE—3-Window. 2P. Models 40,
Type 720.

Windshield	14x42
Door	14x32
Back	10x32

COUPE—5-Window. 2P. Models 40,

Windshield	14x42
Door	14x28
Quarter	12x14
Back	10x32

*Cut to Size. No Pattern Required.

1934

ROADSTER—DeLuxe. Model 40.
Type 710. V-8.

PHAETON—DeLuxe. Model 40.
Type 750. V-8.

Windshield	12x44
*Back ($23\frac{3}{4}$x$3\frac{15}{16}$) ($1\frac{3}{8}$" R. Cors.)	4x24

COUPE—Standard. 3-Window. 2P. Model 40.
Type 720.

Windshield	14x42
Door	14x32
Back	10x32

COUPE—Standard. 5-Window. 2-4P. Model 40.
Type 770.

Windshield	14x42
Door	14x26
Quarter	12x14
Back	10x32

CABRIOLET—Convertible. Model 40.
Type 760. V-8.

Windshield	14x42
Door	14x32
*Back ($23\frac{7}{8}$x$3\frac{15}{16}$) (1" R. Cors.)	4x24

TUDOR SEDAN—2D-5P. Standard and DeLuxe.
Model 40.
Type 700. V-8.

VICTORIA—2D-5P. Model 40.
Type 740. V-8.

Windshield 14x42
Door 16x32
Quarter (Tudor Sedan)...............16x34
Quarter (Victoria) 16x28
Back 10x32

FORDOR SEDAN—4D-5P. Standard and DeLuxe.
Model 40.
Type 730. V-8.

Windshield 14x42
Front Door 16x26
Rear Door 16x26
Quarter 16x16
Back 10x32

*Cut to Size. No Pattern Required.

─────────1935─────────

COUPE—3-Window,
Type 720

Windshield 16x44
Door 14x32
Back 12x32

COUPE—5-Window, Standard, DeLuxe,
Type 770

Windshield 16x44
Door 14x28
Quarter 12x14
Back 12x32

CABRIOLET—2-4P., Standard, DeLuxe,
Type 760

Note: Two different sized door lights.
Windshield 14x44
Door 14x36
Door 14x36
*Back (24x4¾) (1⅜" R. Cors.),........ 6x24

TUDOR—2D-5P., Standard, DeLuxe,
Type 700

Windshield 16x44
Door 14x34
Quarter (Early 1935)................14x34
Quarter (Late 1935) 14x34
Back 10x32

FORDOR—4D-5P., Standard, DeLuxe,
Type 730

Windshield 16x44
Front Door..........................14x28
Rear Door 14x26
Quarter 14x16
Back 10x32

SEDAN—Convertible,
Type 740

Windshield 14x44
Front Door 14x30
Rear Door 14x26
*Back (24x4¾) (1⅜" R. Cors.)........ 6x24

STATION WAGON
Type 790,
Windshield 14x44
Door 16x30

ROADSTER— 2-4P., Body Type 710, V-8.

PHAETON— 5P., Body Type 750, V-8.
Windshield 14x44
*Back (24x4¾) (1⅜" R. Cors.)........ 6x24

*Cut to Size. No Pattern Required.

─────────1936─────────

COUPE—3-Window, Model 68,
Type 720,
Windshield 16x44
Door 14x32
Back 12x32

COUPE—5-Window, Standard and DeLuxe,
Model 68,
Type 770,
Windshield 16x44
Door 14x28
Quarter 12x14
Back 12x32

CABRIOLET—Convertible, Model 68,
Type 760.
Windshield 14x44
Door 14x36
Back 6x24

TUDOR—Standard and DeLuxe, Model 68,
Type 700.
Windshield 16x44
Door 14x34
Quarter 14x34
Back 10x32

FORDOR—Standard, DeLuxe, Model 68,
Type 730.
Windshield 16x44
Front Door 14x28
Rear Door 14x26
Quarter (Flipper) 12x14
Back 10x32

SEDAN—Convertible, 4-D., Model 68,
Type 740.
Windshield 14x44
Front Door 14x30
Rear Door 14x26
Back 6x24

STATION WAGON—
Type 790,
Windshield 14x44
Door 16x30

ROADSTER—Rumble Seat, Model 68,
Type 710,

PHAETON— Model 68,
Type 750, V-8.
Windshield 14x44
Back 6x24

—1937—

STATION WAGON— Model 78,

 Type 790.

Windshield (2)	14x22
Front Door	16x30
Rear Door (DeLuxe)	14x16
Quarter Front (DeLuxe)	16x22
Quarter Rear	16x24
Back	10x52

1938-1939

STATION WAGON—DeLuxe, Models 81C, 91A,

 Types 790 and 79.

Windshield (2)	14x22
Front Door	16x30
Rear Door (2 Piece)	14x16
Quarter Front	16x22
Quarter Rear	16x24
Back	10x52

STATION WAGON—Standard, Models 82C, 91A,

 Types 790 and 79.

Windshield (2)	14x22
Front Door	16x30
Other Openings Not Glass.	

1937-1938

COUPE—Club. Models 78, 81A,

 Type 720.

Windshield (2)	14x22
Wing (Special Equipment)	8x16
Door	14x34
Quarter (Flipper)	12x18
Back (2)	12x18

1937-1938-1939

CABRIOLET—Models 78, 81A, 91A,

 Types 760-A-B and 76B.

ROADSTER—Models 78,

 Types 710

PHAETON— Models 78, 81A,

 Type 750

Windshield (2)	14x22
Door (Cabriolet)	14x36
Back	6x20

COUPE—5 Window, Standard and DeLuxe,

 Models 74, 78, 81A, 82A, 91A,

 Types 770, 770-A-B, 77-A-B.

Windshield (2)	14x22
Wing (Special Equipment)	8x16
Door	14x28
Quarter	12x16
Back (2)	12x18

TUDOR—2D-5P., Touring, Standard and DeLuxe,

 Models 74, 78; 81A, 82A; 91A, 922A.

 Types 700-A-B-C-D, 70A, 70B.

Windshield (2)	14x22
Wing (Special Equipment)	8x16
Door (1937-38-39 Standard & DeLuxe)	14x34
Quarter (1937 Standard & DeLuxe 74, 78)	14x34
Quarter (1938 Standard 82A)	14x34
Quarter (1938 DeLuxe 81A)	14x36
Quarter (1939 Standard, DeLuxe 91A, 922A)	14x36
Back (1937 Standard & DeLuxe) (2)	12x18
Back (1938 Standard 82A) (2)	12x18
Back (1938 DeLuxe 81A) (2)	14x16
Back (1939 Standard & DeLuxe) (2)	14x16

FORDOR—4D-5P., Touring, Standard and DeLuxe,

 Models 74, 78, 81A, 82A, 91A,

 Types 730, 730- A-B-C-D, 73A, 73B.

 With Trunk.

Windshield (2)	14x22
Wing (Special Equipment)	8x16
Front Door	14x28
Rear Door	14x24
Quarter (Sta.) (1937 Standard and DeLuxe)	12x16
Quarter (Flipper) (1937 Standard and DeLuxe	12x12
Quarter (Stationary) (1938 Standard)	12x16
Quarter (Flipper) (1938-1939 DeLuxe)	10x20
Quarter (Stationary) (1939 Standard)	12x22
Back (2) (1937 Standard & DeLuxe)	12x18
Back (2) (1938 Standard)	12x18
Back (2) (1938 DeLuxe)	14x16
Back (2) (1939 Standard & DeLuxe)	14x16

SEDAN—4D. Convertible, DeLuxe,

 Models 78, 81A, 91A,

 Types 740 and 74.

Windshield (2)	14x22
Front Door	14x30
Rear Door	14x26
Back	6x20

—1940—

COUPE-—Club Convertible, DeLuxe Model 01A,

 Type 66, Five Passenger.

Windshield (2)	14x22
Door Vent	10x12
Door	14x24
Back	6x20

COUPE—Business, Standard Model 01A.

 Type 67A-B,

 5 Window, DeLuxe Model 01A,

 Type 77A-B.

Windshield (2) (Standard Equipment)	16x24
Windshield (2) (Ventilating Optional)	14x22
Door Vent	10x12
Door	14x18
Quarter	12x16
Back (2)	12x18

TUDOR—2D-5P., Standard and DeLuxe, Model 01A.

Types 70A, B.

Windshield (2) (Standard Equipment) 16x24
Windshield (2) (Ventilating Optional) 14x22
Door Vent..........................10x12
Door 14x24
Quarter 14x36
Back (2) 14x16

FORDOR—4D-5P., Standard and DeLuxe, Model 01A.

Type 73-A-B.

Windshield (2) (Standard Equipment) 16x24
Windshield (2) (Ventilating Optional) 14x22
Front Door Vent...................10x12
Front Door ....:.14x18
Rear Door 14x24
Quarter (Stationary) (Standard)....12x22
Quarter (Flipper) (DeLuxe)........10x20
Back (2) 14x16

STATION WAGON—Standard and DeLuxe, Model 01A,

Types 79A and 79B.

Windshield (2) 14x22
Front Door 16x30
Rear Door (2 piece)...............14x16
Quarter Front 16x22
Quarter Rear 16x26
Back (Standard) 10x52
Back (2) (DeLuxe).................10x24

————————1941————————

COUPE—DeLuxe, Super DeLuxe, 11A.

Types 67A, 67B.

Auxiliary Seat 5 Window,

Types 77A, 77B, 77C.

Windshield (2) 18x26
Door Vent.........................10x12
Door 16x18
Quarter 14x22
Back (Bent) 14x34

SEDAN-COUPE—Super DeLuxe, Model 11A.

Type 72.

Windshield (2) 18x26
Door Vent.........................10x12
Door 16x28
Quarter 14x20
Back (Bent) 14x34

COUPE—Club, Convertible, Super DeLuxe, Model 11A,

Type 76.

Windshield (2) 18x26
Door Vent.........................12x14
Door 16x26
Back 8x22

TUDOR—DeLuxe, Super DeLuxe, Special. Model 11A.

Types 70A, B, C.

Windshield (2) 18x26
Door Vent.........................10x12
Door 16x28
Quarter 18x38
Back (Bent) 14x34

FORDOR—DeLuxe, Super DeLuxe, Special. Model 11A.

Types 73A, B, C.

Windshield (2) 18x26
Front Door Vent...................10x12
Front Door 16x18
Rear Door 16x28
Quarter (Flipper) (Super DeLuxe)..12x20
Quarter (Stationary)
(DeLuxe Special) 14x22
Back (Bent) 14x34

STATION WAGON—DeLuxe and Super DeLuxe. Model 11A.

Types 79A, B.

Windshield (2) 18x26
Front Door Vent...................10x12
Front Door 16x18
Rear Door (2 piece)...............14x16
Quarter Front 16x22
Quarter Rear 16x26
Back (2) 12x26

————————1942————————

COUPE—DeLuxe, Super DeLuxe, Models 2GA, 21A.

Types 77A, B, C. Business, 5 Window

Windshield (2) 18x26
Door Vent.........................10x12
Door (1st Series Bar Sliding)........16x18
Door (2nd Series Bar Stationary)....16x18
Quarter 14x22
Back (Bent) 14x34

SEDAN-COUPE—DeLuxe and Super DeLuxe. Models 21A, 2GA.

Types 72A, B.

Windshield (2) 18x26
Door Vent.........................10x12
Door (1st Series Bar Sliding)........16x28
Door (2nd Series Bar Stationary)....16x28
Quarter (DeLuxe) 11x22
Quarter (Super DeLuxe)...........14x20
Back (Bent) 14x34

COUPE—Club Convertible. Super DeLuxe. Models 2GA, 21A.

Type 76.

Windshield (2) 18x26
Door Vent.........................12x14
Door 16x26
Quarter 14x20
Back 8x22

TUDOR—DeLuxe, Super DeLuxe Models 2GA, 21A.

Types 70A, B

Windshield (2) 18x26
Door Vent.........................10x12
Door (1st Series Bar Sliding)........16x28
Door (2nd Series Bar Stationary)....16x28
Quarter 18x38
Back (Bent) 14x34

FORDOR—DeLuxe, Super DeLuxe Models 2GA, 21A.

Types 73A, B

Windshield (2) 18x26
Front Door Vent...................10x12
Front Door (1st Series Bar Sliding)..16x18
Front Door (2nd Series Bar
Stationary) 16x18
Rear Door 16x28
Quarter (Flipper) Super DeLuxe.....12x20
Quarter (Stationary) DeLuxe, ...14x22
Back (Bent) 14x34

STATION WAGON—Super DeLuxe, Models 2GA, 21A,

Type 79B.

Windshield (2) 18x26
Front Door Vent...................10x12
Front Door 16x18
Rear Door (1 Piece)...............18x28
Quarter Front 16x22
Quarter Rear 16x26
Back (2) 12x26

FORD MOTOR COMPANY PASSENGER CAR PRODUCTION

	Domestic	Canada	Foreign	Total
1932*	287,285	19,975	12,986	320,246
1933*	334,969	19,094	39,219	393,282
1934*	563,921	35,376	42,124	641,421
1935	942,439	58,500	57,722	1,058,661
1936	791,812	42,861	94,905	929,578
1937	848,608	48,618	111,527	1,008,753
1938	410,048	48,429	89,002	547,479
1939	532,152	41,072	69,707	642,931
1940	599,175	32,486	10,919	642,580
1941*	600,814	26,880	1,869	629,563
1942*	43,407	4,442	853	48,702
1943	0	0	40	40
	5,954,630	377,733	530,873	6,863,236

*includes four-cylinder engine in 1932-1934 and six-cylinder in 1941-42

. . .from FORD: DECLINE & REBIRTH 1933-1962 by Nevins & Hill,
Charles Scribner's Sons